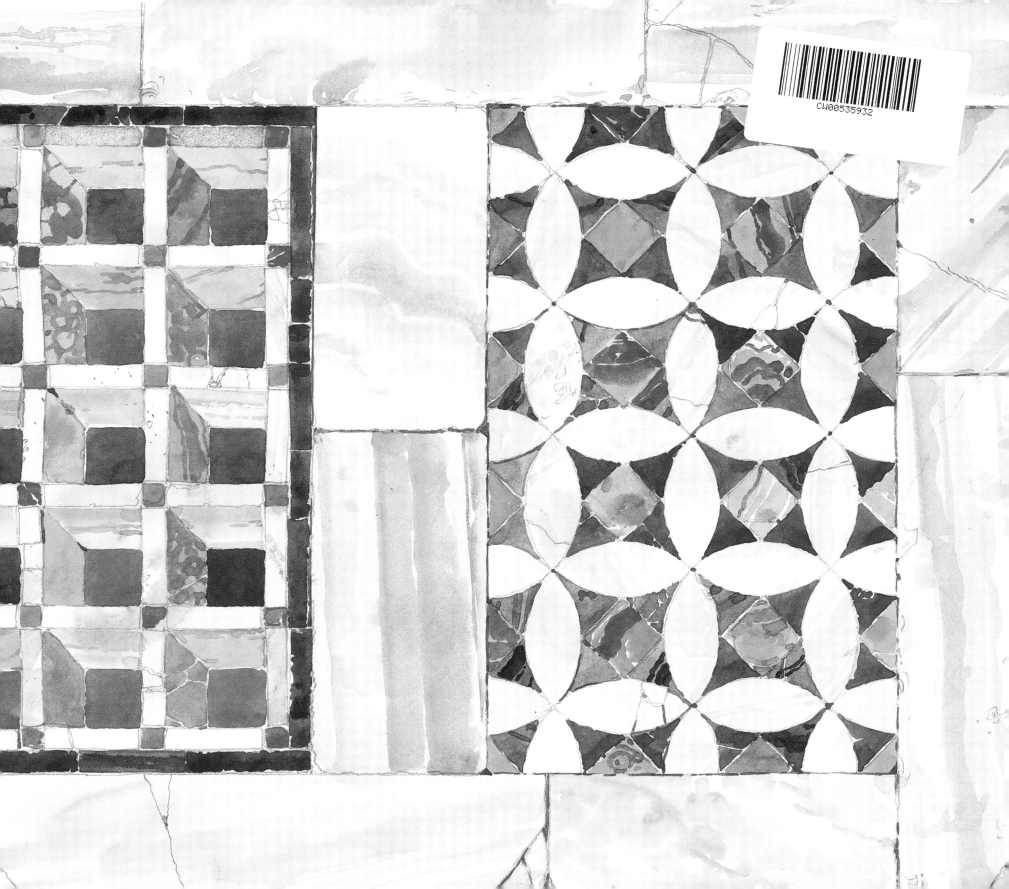

Venice

Sketchbook

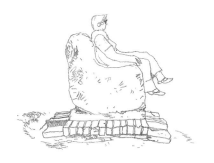

*To Valérie,
Alice and Émile*

Front cover: the Grand Canal.
Front flap: Campiello delle Erbe, near San Polo.
Back cover: Venise from San Giorgio Maggiore's campanile.

The publisher wishes to thank Barry Winkleman, Alexandra Keen,
Alessandro et Francesca Vattani, for their valuable collaboration.
Fabrice Moireau wishes to thank Mrs Lorenzon, Ines Bragato, Patricia Curtis-Vigano,
Alberto Tozzo and Davide Salvatore, Guerrino Lovato, Giovanni Alliata (Fondation Cini),
Franca Sacerdoti, Mr and Mrs A. Barnabo, Jagoda Buic, Etaliza Basaldella.

Text and captions translated from the French by Philippa Richmond.

Paintings © Fabrice Moireau
Text, design and typography © Éditions du Pacifique, 2004

First published in French as *Venise Aquarelles* in 2004 by Les Éditions du Pacifique
5, rue Saint-Romain, 75006 Paris

Colour separation by Sang Choy, Singapore
Printing by Star Standard, Singapore

ISBN 10: 0-312-334583-0
ISBN 13: 978-0-312-33458-1
First U.S. Edition: November 2004
Reprinted in 2007.

Venice
Sketchbook

Paintings Fabrice Moireau

Introduction Deborah Howard

Text Tudy Sammartini

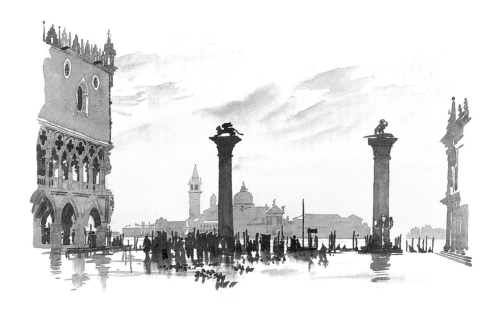

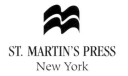

ST. MARTIN'S PRESS
New York

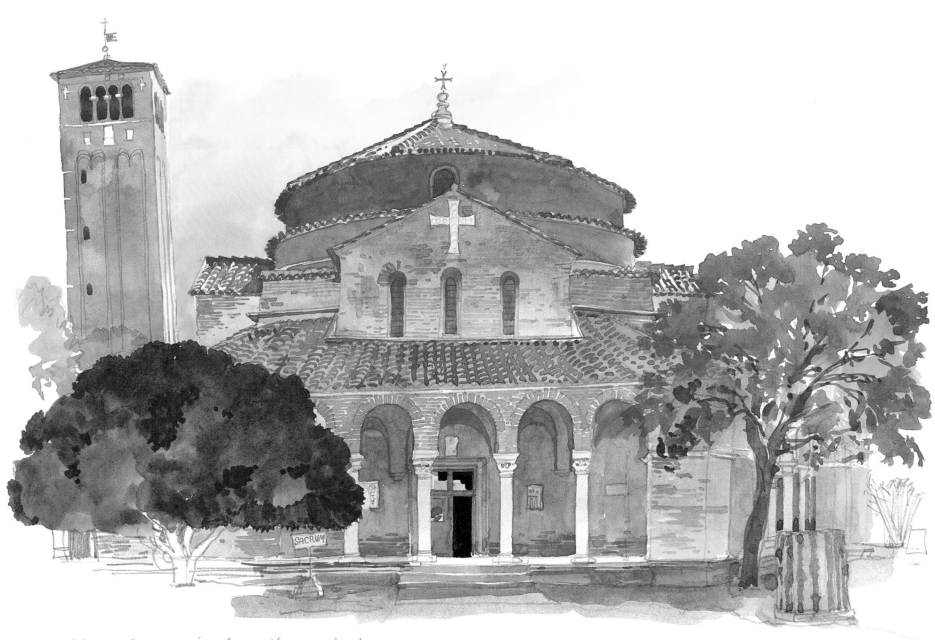

Venetians still love the ancient
church of Santa Fosca on the island of Torcello;
on most Sundays it is filled with
white flowers and local people for a wedding —
much to the joy of passing tourists.

Contents

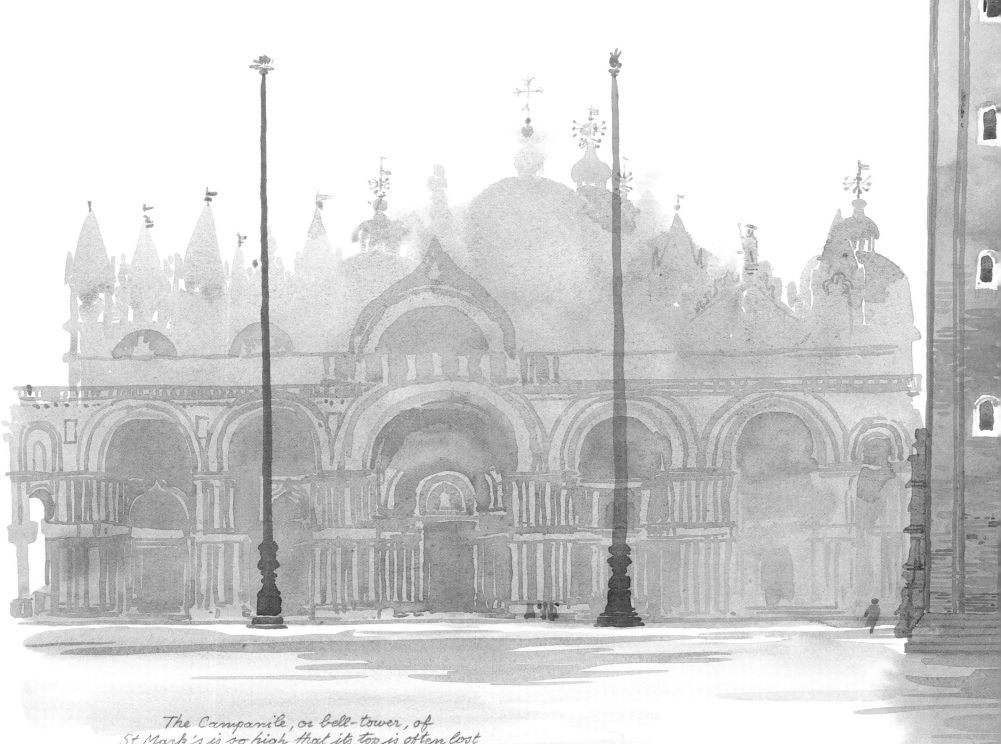

The Campanile, or bell-tower, of
St Mark's is so high that its top is often lost
in cloud. Together with three tall, red flagstaffs,
it stands like a shield in front of the church, blurred
by the freezing fog of an early winter's morning.

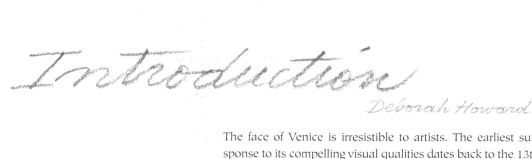

Introduction

Deborah Howard

The face of Venice is irresistible to artists. The earliest surviving response to its compelling visual qualities dates back to the 13th century: on the far left lunette of the façade of St Mark's, a glittering image of the church from around 1260 is the sole survivor of a narrative that once ran across all five bays. Ever since that time, mosaicists, draughtsmen, painters, print-makers and cartographers have exercised their skills in pictorial description, documenting every facet of the city's townscape. Artists such as Gentile Bellini, Carpaccio and Canaletto recorded its appearance in intricate detail. Their painstaking attention to minutiae – from the ordinary to the remarkable – created timeless settings for the ephemera of everyday life. Guardi and Turner, by contrast, explored the more transient effects of light and colour.

Different media suit different modes of depiction: flickering mosaics recall the icon-like, hieratic quality of Byzantine art; the deep glow of oil painting evokes the translucent glow of rich oriental marbles; and the linear precision of prints caresses the intricately carved detail of Gothic traceries. But perhaps no medium is better fitted than watercolour to capture the play of light as it flickers between sky, water and man-made artefacts.

In Venice, all five senses receive constant stimulation. Most obviously, as if in vanity, the city demands visual scrutiny from the viewer. The slow pace of pedestrian and water traffic allows the city-dweller and visitor alike to observe the city without the distractions of the paraphernalia of traffic. Even the most blasé passer-by can hardly fail to react to the sudden revelation of the snow-capped Dolomites seen from the Fondamente Nuove on a crisp, cold day, or to the spooky gloom of a winter fog. On a clear, sunny day the light can be so intense that supersaturated colours convey a heightened reality. Venice seems to burn in its unforgettable sunsets. In more humid conditions, shades are softened and blended by haze, or turned to uniform greyish brown by relentless rain. From the large scale of distant vistas to the close range of curious details, Venice entices the brush, the pen and the camera alike.

Similarly, the ear becomes more responsive in the absence of traffic noise. The sounds of the city, like its visual images, are distinctive and evocative. Ambient noise is punctuated by the lapping of water, the sombre resonance of church bells, the chugging of vaporetti, echoing footsteps in narrow alleys, or the soft sing-song of Venetian dialect. The twisted rope around the cleat of a boat-stop yields the unmistakeable creaking sound of jute rubbing against metal. All these noises involve

To the south, next to the
island of Pellestrina, the lagoon
is given over entirely to fishing
huge mussel beds stretch as
far as the eye can see.

movement, often in a gently swaying rhythm that is reflected in many of the musical compositions inspired by the city.

With less pollution from petrol fumes, even the nose is sensitised. The city's characteristic smells can yield unexpected whiffs of nostalgia. Among the most evocative are those that also stimulate the taste-buds, such as the baking of early-morning croissants or frying fish at noon. But even the odours of damp bricks, stagnant canals or stale fog can trigger poignant memories.

What about touch? Favourite tactile sensations range from the cold terrazzo floor under the bare foot in summer to the soothing warmth of a sun-kissed stone parapet in spring. Some of the less pleasant experiences, such as the jostling crowds in the Merceria on a hot, sticky day seem to be problems provoked by modern tourism, but in reality the Merceria has always teemed with cosmopolitan hoards of pedestrians, and summers have always been hot and humid.

Venice seems to heighten the body's sensual responses. Perhaps the slower pace of life gives one more time to reflect on physical sensations. The seasons and times of day are sensed more vividly than from a bus or car. Pedestrians observe each other, and those strolling in Piazza San Marco, on the Zattere or the Riva degli Schiavoni seem conscious of being watched. The relationship between spectator and spectacle can be oddly ambiguous: a person gazing from a Grand Canal balcony is, in turn, subject to observation by those in the boats below. Carnival brings hoards of posers in fancy dress, but even the locals showing off their tans on the beach at Lido or gathering in the foyer of the opera seem to expect to be noticed.

Historically the frontiers between public and private space in Venice have been surprisingly blurred. Venice has a strong tradition of public service: for eleven centuries it was governed as a Republic, the longest-lasting the world has ever known. During the lifetime of the Republic its inhabitants could wander freely into the courtyard of the Doge's Palace, and even draw water from its two wells, despite the building's triple function as ducal residence, communal palace and law courts. The central halls of the great palaces of the nobility could be penetrated by the gaze of the passer-by, especially at night when their huge, multi-light windows revealed ornate Murano glass chandeliers and richly painted ceilings. A curious corollary was the fascination with anonymity in public space – masks and covered gondolas provided the ideal cover for clandestine encounters, for gambling, flirting or intrigue.

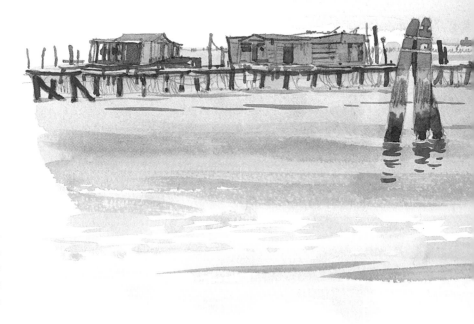

Every one wants Venice for him/herself, yet the city has always depended on people – both visitors and inhabitants. Tourism is not new to Venice. Already by the 15th century, Venice had established a thriving package-tour business shipping pilgrims to the Holy Land. This tourist trade was strictly regulated by the state, who determined the dates of departure of the pilgrim galleys, often delayed for unspecified reasons so that the faithful could visit the holy sites of Venice and buy necessities for their voyage.

How did this extraordinary city come into being? A more unpropitious site for building could scarcely be imagined. Founded during the final collapse of the Roman Empire on an archipelago of marshy islands

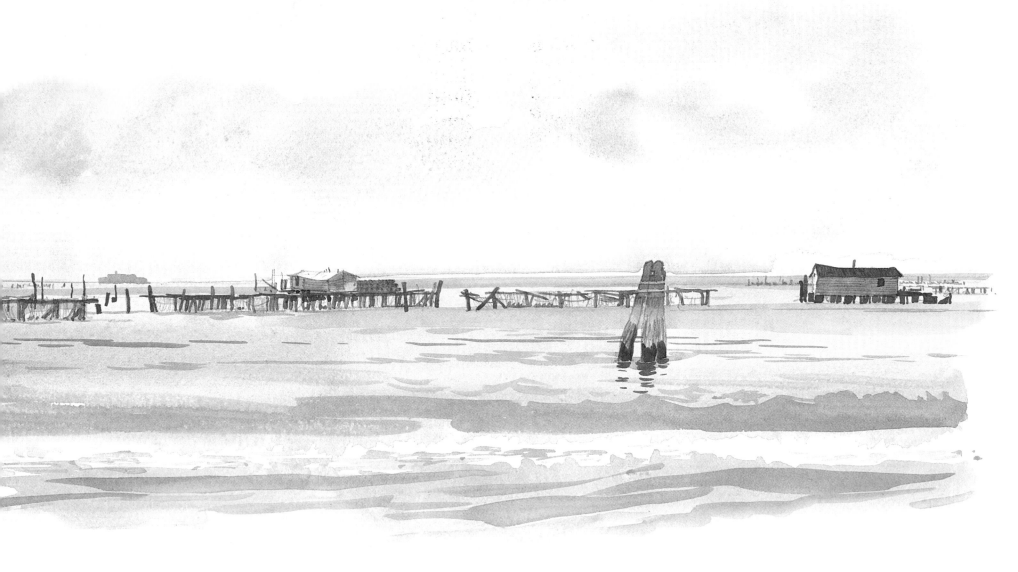

in a shallow lagoon, Venice's foundation myth dated the city's inception to the year AD 421. In the amphibious terrain lay the secret of the city's self-defence: until the Republic finally submitted to Napoleonic forces in 1797, the 'virgin city' was never violated by invaders.

The earliest settlements on scattered marshy islands gradually coalesced, thanks to piecemeal land reclamation, to form a more coherent land mass. Although most drainage schemes were private initiatives, each had to be approved by the state authorities, who ultimately had the power to control the shape of the city. The islands settled earliest grew in an organic, cellular pattern, whereas later reclamations, such as northern Cannaregio, appear more rectilinear, thanks to the uniform dimensions

of the individual parcels for which reclamation consent was granted.

Water has endowed the city with its most precious asset. Over the centuries, sophisticated hydraulic engineering works prevented the natural silting up of the lagoon, in order to protect the city's trading arteries. Until the drainage or covering of many canals under Austrian domination in the 19th century, every major dwelling and commercial building had both land and water access. Even today canals penetrate the whole surface of the city, still delineating some of the original parish boundaries. In a curious prototype of the planning utopias of modernism, heavy traffic uses a completely separate network of arteries from pedestrians. Rarely can one walk along the waterways, in contrast to,

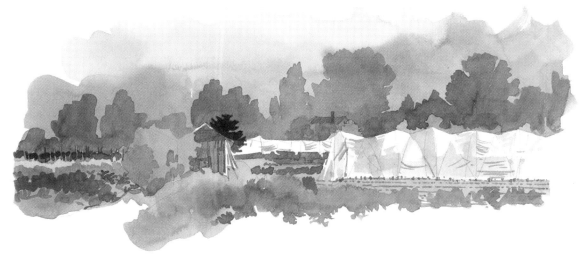

say, Amsterdam. The Grand Canal must be the only major street in the world lacking in pavements for most of its length. In contrast to the dark confines of the narrow streets, the lagoon frontages reveal dazzling vistas and shimmering surfaces.

Light and colour are freely exchanged between water and buildings, as Monet so brilliantly recognised in his Venetian pictures. Flickering sunlight on the water projects its ripples on to the undersides of bridges. Other reflections can be almost photographic in their perfect, upside-down realism. Flapping laundry over a canal can paint the water surface with a bewildering array of trousers, sheets and underwear. Water reflects light upwards, an effect which encouraged the stonemasons of the past to embellish the undersides of architectural elements such as balconies, portals or gutters. In the absence of landscape, only water softens and enlivens the building fabric, its impact constantly changing according to the weather or time of day. On the water, the horizon shifts constantly and the world is seen in perpetual motion. Boats allow one to be either lazy or energetic, for rowing is the Venetians' favourite form of exercise.

Yet the waterlogged shifting sands on which the city was erected demanded ingenious building technology. Swilled by the rise and fall of the tides, the subsoil is soft and unstable. Most buildings, in effect, 'float' on rafts over pile foundations pegged into the loose mud, with their weight distributed as evenly as possible to avoid differential subsidence. Contrary to our modern perceptions that structures should be rigid and watertight, in Venice buildings need both flexibility and 'breathability'. Lightweight brick walls, bonded with traditional lime mortar, can survive a degree of deformation, while being porous enough for moisture to evaporate. The rich red terracotta colour of the local bricks gives the townscape its characteristic palette, matching the warm colour of the crinkly clay roof-tiles.

The rough, rusty brickwork is offset by crisp white detailing in Istrian stone. This remarkable material was one of Venice's greatest resources. Following the annexation of Istria (now part of Slovenia) in the 14th century, the city's masons extracted its pure white limestone, to be shipped straight to the building site from the seaside quarries. The stone's impermeability made it the ideal material for a range of crucial uses. Although it has the same chemical composition as marble, Istrian stone has a more even, fine-grained texture, ideal for carving into intricate detail. As if embroidered like lace, it could be wrought into ornate Gothic window traceries; later, it proved ideal for exuberant Baroque caryatids, fierce keystone heads and knobbly balustrades. Istrian stone gutters, often lovingly decorated on the underside, encircled the wall-heads to collect every possible drop of water from the hipped roofs. Istrian stone damp-courses protected the walls from rising damp (until the city's subsidence in the post-war period made most of these redundant). From the Renaissance onwards, whole façades were often clad in a veneer of Istrian stone, applied over the brick core. The same stone could even protect the corner of a building against carelessly steered boats.

Red and white are thus the traditional hues of the Venetian townscape, although stuccoes in a wide range of other colours – such as Sienese yellow ochre and pale coral – are now making their impact. Originally brick walls were protected with a very thin layer of intonaco, made of brick dust or crushed marble. As these stuccoes peeled off, the walls acquired a random surface, with picturesquely varied hues and textures. Today's new stucco finishes are often much thicker, more impervious and less flexible than the traditional types. The consequences of such heavy-handed restoration have yet to be assessed.

Wood was a precious material in Venice, for its use in vast quantities for shipbuilding pushed up the price. Builders clearly distinguished between different kinds of wood. Oak was the favourite timber for pile foundations, becoming almost petrified by constant submersion. For ceilings and roof timbers, softwoods such as pine and fir were cheaper (being faster growing), lighter in weight, more flexible, and more resistant to damp thanks to their high resin content. The most beautiful softwood was larch, with a distinctively patterned grain that could also be reproduced in paint on cheaper wood. Wooden doors and beams were often lovingly carved, as if in recognition of the scarcity and preciousness of the material. The exchange of expertise between the separate guilds of ships' carpenters and house joiners allowed the construction

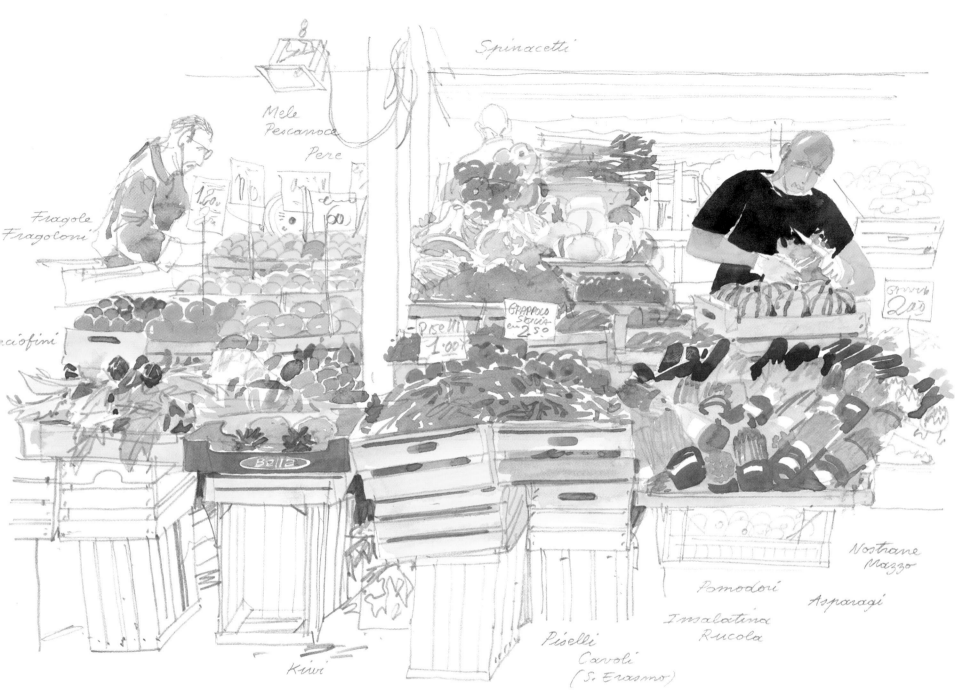

Spinacetti

Mele
Pescanoca
Pere

Fragole
Fragoloni

ciofini

ciofini

GRAPPOLO STORIA
en 2.50

PISELLI
1.00

Balle

Kiwi

Banane

Piselli
Cavoli
(S. Erasmo)

Insalatina
Rucola

Pomodori

Nostrane
Mazzo

Asparagi

At dawn, boats laden with fruit and
vegetables leave Sant'Erasmo, to the east of Venice,
bringing their wares to the central market in
the Rialto. The stalls are a colourful spectacle,
satisfying to all the senses.
But how much longer will rocket, chicory,
courgettes and other such delicacies
be sold here?

A mask of Sigismondo Malatesta da Rimini, the heroic "condottiere" (general) who received a sword wound on his nose; it is based on Piero della Francesca's famous portrait.

A 16th-century doctor's mask – for protection against the plague!

Christopher Columbus. In the wake of Marco Polo, he discovered America

The mask of the short-sighted stutterer, a figure from mediaeval fable later adopted by the Commedia dell' arte.

of the beautiful ship's-keel ceilings still to be seen in Venetian churches such as Santo Stefano and San Giacomo dall'Orio. Wood was also in demand as a heating fuel, a fact which led to the invention of ingenious chimney pots designed to trap cinders – some like upturned cones, others arranged like small flights of steps.

From earliest times, glass was among Venice's most famous industries thanks to the profusion of its main raw material, sand, and the acquisition of technological expertise from the east. If we are to believe the author of the first guide-book to the city by Francesco Sansovino, published in 1581, even the simplest houses had glass windows by this time. The existence of glass was essential to protect the great palace halls or 'porteghi' from the elements. Composed of small discs of bottle-glass set in lead, windows turned the view of the city outside into a shimmering mosaic, filtered by the faintly tinted colours of the individual panes. Shutters, usually painted in dark green, change the relationship of light to dark in a façade when open or closed. Similarly, at night, a façade turns into a photographic negative of itself – or so this used to be before the city's population began to leak away.

During the past thirty years, the population of the city has halved, leading to radical social and demographic changes. In order to understand the relationship between the fabric of the city and the structure of its society, it is therefore necessary, regrettably, to speak in the past tense, and even to refer to the traditional society of the Republic before its collapse in 1797. Before the Napoleonic reorganisation, each of the seventy islands formed a separate parish, centred on the parochial church and its campo (literally a field). Beneath the campo a huge cistern stored water for the public well; the positions of the drains that led the water underground are often still visible, even if capped by stone discs. The parish address gave identity to its occupants – indeed, many women rarely left the confines of the parish. The residential quarters were labyrinthine enclaves, densely built up like a traditional Islamic

city, with only occasional glimpses into private courtyards or gardens. Although some parishes were wealthier than others, all contained a broad social mix of inhabitants, including a few families from the nobility, some cittadini or middle-class inhabitants, larger numbers of skilled artisans, and even more unskilled workers.

In such a densely built-up topography, skyline elements are crucial for establishing one's position. These may be statues, altane (wooden rooftop terraces supported on brick piers), campanili (belfries), pointed dormer windows, idiosyncratic chimneys, or bulging domes topped by open iron-work baubles. Interspersed with these are the intrusions of television aerials and satellite dishes. Campanili were used for navigation by ocean-going ships, many portolan atlases giving verbal rather than diagrammatic instructions.

Until the 19th century, all Venetian dwellings, even the great palaces that flank the Grand Canal, were simply called houses, that is, 'case' or 'ca' ' for short. The only exception was the Doge's Palace, just as the only 'piazza' was Piazza San Marco. By the 14th century, a standardised typology had evolved for the palaces of the nobility, based on the formula of a deep plan and a structure of four parallel

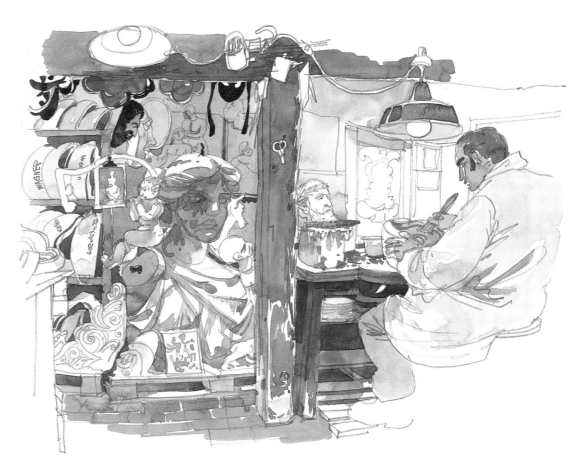

spine walls running from front to back. On each floor, the central hall served as the main circulation space or 'portego', lit by huge multi-light windows at either end. Here portraits and military trophies were displayed, Venetian ladies took exercise, and wedding feasts were held. Smaller rooms on either side provided private apartments for different family members. On sites hemmed in by other buildings, a small light-well might be inserted into one of the side wings, although the favourite position for the main courtyard was at the landward end of the site. Here a clay-lined cistern stored rainwater collected both from the roof and from the surface of the courtyard, filtered through terracotta pipes and sand to supply a clean source of drinking water. Over the cistern stood a 'vera da pozzo' or well-head, often formed like a giant capital, as if pillaged from the ruins of some ancient Roman city. Family coats of arms asserted lineage and ownership on well-heads and portals.

Venetians loved to insert pieces of sculpture brought from elsewhere into the external walls of their houses. These trophies, engagingly called 'sculture erratiche' like erratic boulders swept up by glacial moraine, document the centuries of trading voyages that criss-crossed the Mediterranean. Some fragments were treasured for their rare coloured marbles, others for their curious carvings or family associations. Indeed, just as the markets of Venice accumulated a dazzling variety of rare spices, textiles, dyes and aromatics from eastern destinations, so too, the city's architecture, culture and language absorbed myriad elements from far-away destinations. The eclecticism of the city's self-image was fused into a strong local traditional identity, modulated over time, but always proud of the range of associations from outside, and alert to their connotations and intended meanings. Some sculptures seem almost theatrical, like the eccentric statues of orientals inserted into the walls of a house near the church of the Madonna dell'Orto, which seem like petrified characters from a comic opera. Apparently refashioned from religious statuary by the addition of outsized turbans, these figures probably allude to the trading activities of the owner of the house, who was a spice-merchant.

Trade and the manufacture of luxury goods such as glass and textiles still make their mark on the city. Traditional shop-fronts are framed by hefty Istrian-stone piers, each topped by a broad wooden lintel protected from the rain by a small stone ledge. Vegetable sellers display their produce arranged in a brilliant palette of colour at the edge of the pavement, and fishmongers ply their wares noisily at the Rialto market. In the neo-

Gothic Pescaria or fish market, built in 1907, a series of irreverent capitals display various species of fish. One can still peep into the workshops of skilled artisans such as furniture restorers and blacksmiths.

The art of boat-building survives in the few remaining 'squeri' or boatyards. The impressive former state shipyards of the Arsenal are best visited during the Biennale when their cavernous spaces host installations of art and architecture. The largest industrial complex in medieval Europe, the Arsenal even made its appearance in Dante's Inferno (canto XXI), where the great vats of boiling pitch for caulking provided the perfect imagery for the horrors of hell. The former rope-works, known as the 'Tana', have a continuous aisled interior over 300 metres long. At the land entrance to the Arsenal a Roman-style triumphal arch, built soon after the Fall of Constantinople to the Ottomans in 1453, re-uses Byzantine capitals, as if to claim the inheritance of Byzantium. On either side, ancient Greek statues of lions, brought to Venice at various dates, further assert Venice's links with the Eastern Mediterranean. The Arsenal enclave is the only sizeable area of Venice to be protected by fortifications.

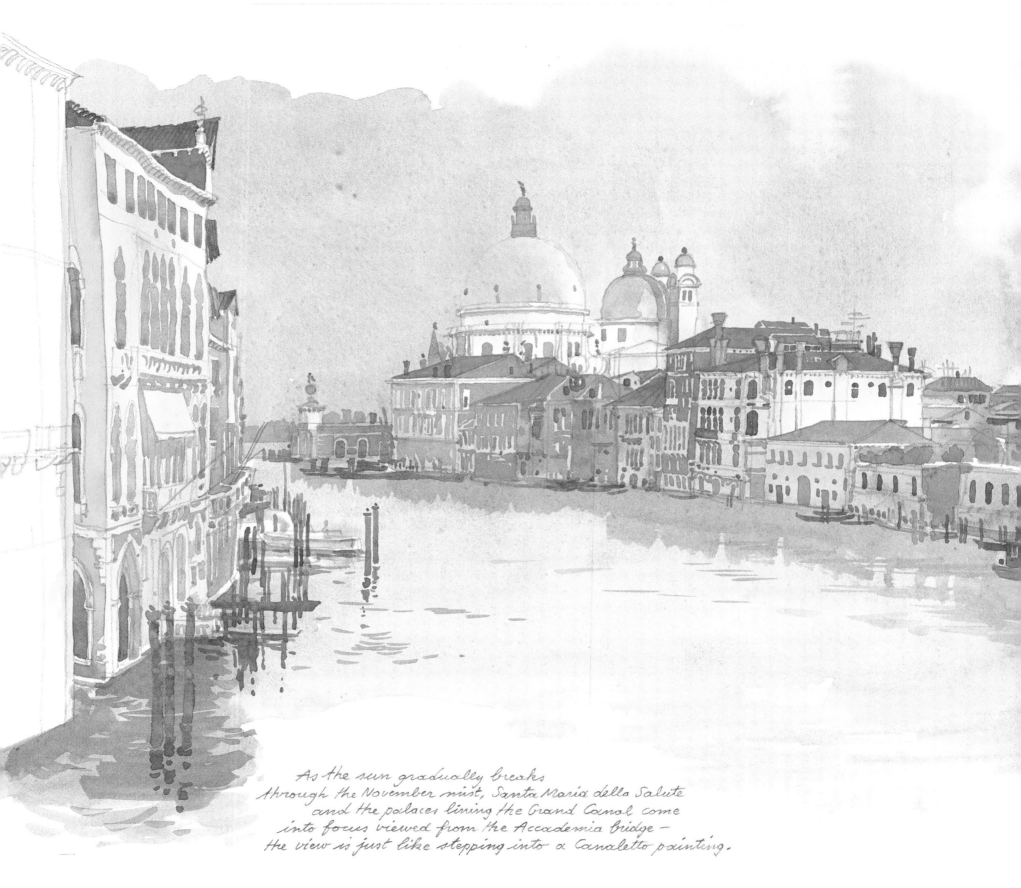

As the sun gradually breaks
through the November mist, Santa Maria della Salute
and the palaces lining the Grand Canal come
into focus viewed from the Accademia bridge —
the view is just like stepping into a Canaletto painting.

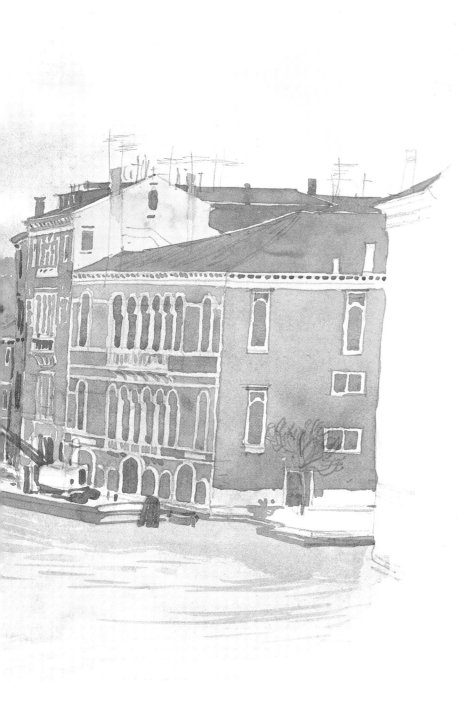

Because of its island site and treacherous shallow waterways, Venice had no need of the great ramparts that protected most great European cities. Thus its edges were open to view, and the visitor could arrive in the very heart of the city, between the pair of columns in front of the Doge's Palace. The analogy with the two great columns that stood outside the biblical palace of Solomon would not have gone unnoticed. Solomon's reputation for justice and wisdom gave him the perfect credentials as a role model for the Venetian state. Indeed, the Doge's Palace itself closely resembles many aspects of the description of Solomon's Palace in the first Book of Kings, chapter 7.

Alongside the Doge's Palace rise the five bulbous domes of the church of St Mark's, which housed the relics of Mark the Evangelist, brought to Venice from Alexandria by two Venetian merchants in AD 828/9. St Mark's was not the cathedral of Venice: as if to prevent interference from papal authority, the cathedral of San Pietro di Castello occupies a site at the far eastern end of the city. Instead, St Mark's, the palatine chapel, became the centre of state ceremonial and the hub of the city's devotional life. Solemn processions held on more than sixty occasions in every year carried the elaborate rituals of state out into the open air, as if to remind the public of the power and magnificence of the Republic. Even the special liturgy of St Mark's was taken to other sites on the annual visits made by the Doge to other Venetian churches during the course of the religious calendar.

These two iconic buildings, St Mark's and the Doge's Palace, represent different architectural styles. St Mark's is essentially a Byzantine church, modelled on the venerable five-domed church of the Holy Apostles in Constantinople. The present church was begun under Doge Domenico Contarini in about 1063 and consecrated in 1094. Over the centuries, its interior was lined with mosaics and coloured marbles, and unlike most true Byzantine churches these materials also gradually encrusted the exterior. After the Venetian sacking of Constantinople in the Fourth Crusade of 1204, huge quantities of rare oriental marbles and carved sculptures were shipped to Venice and prominently displayed on the south-facing wall of the basilica. The modern eye is no longer attuned to the origins of different marbles, but the well-informed medieval viewer would have recognised the special qualities of individual stones, savouring the rarity of porphyry and admiring the glossy green of verde antico. The concentration of porphyry columns around the central portal conferred triumphal, imperial associations, while the bays at either

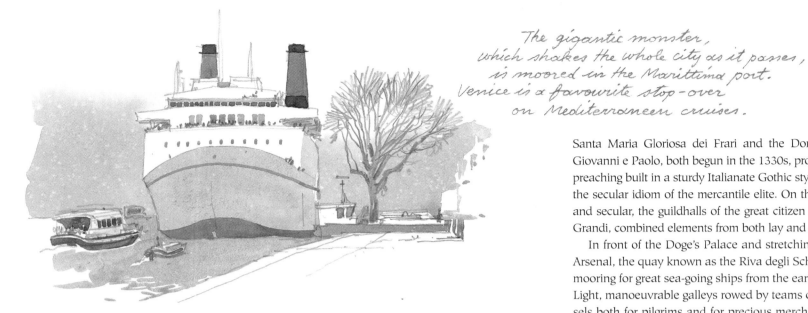

The gigantic monster, which shakes the whole city as it passes, is moored in the Marittima port. Venice is a favourite stop-over on Mediterranean cruises.

end displayed subtly veined marbles in shades of grey and beige, some vertically striated, some spirally veined and some banded horizontally. After the Fourth Crusade Venice began to break away from the Byzantine legacy, embellishing the church with exotic elements borrowed from the Moslem world. Later Gothic accretions elaborated the skyline with cusps, pinnacles and statues.

The Doge's Palace's south wing, begun in 1341 and continued along the west side in the 15th century, draws its stylistic references from a seamless blend of Gothic and Islamic elements, representing the city's two main trading links – the Moslem world and northern Europe. Venice served as a great international emporium where goods from the east could be exchanged with produce from the north. Gothic and Moslem architecture shared many characteristics, from the pointed arch to the love of delicately carved ornament inspired by plant forms. Thus these two styles not only expressed Venice's commercial and cultural connections, but also blended perfectly to create a Venetian architectural vocabulary. So enduring was the image of the Doge's Palace that, when it was seriously damaged by two fires in 1574 and 1577, the government refused Palladio's advise to rebuild it in classical style.

The Gothic period corresponded with Venice's greatest commercial and political success. During the 14th and 15th centuries, Gothic buildings grew up all over the city, as Jacopo de' Barbari's woodcut bird's-eye view of 1500 shows vividly. As the ruling oligarchy sought to define its class identity in bricks and stone, the façades of merchants' palaces adopted the same mix of inspiration from north and east as the Doge's Palace. Meanwhile this style received further stimulus from the arrival of the mendicant orders from mainland Italy. The great churches erected by these new urban religious orders, especially the Franciscan church of

Santa Maria Gloriosa dei Frari and the Dominican church of Santi Giovanni e Paolo, both begun in the 1330s, provided majestic arenas for preaching built in a sturdy Italianate Gothic style, much less ornate than the secular idiom of the mercantile elite. On the cusp between religious and secular, the guildhalls of the great citizen confraternities, or Scuole Grandi, combined elements from both lay and sacred traditions.

In front of the Doge's Palace and stretching eastwards towards the Arsenal, the quay known as the Riva degli Schiavoni became the main mooring for great sea-going ships from the early 14th century onwards. Light, manoeuvrable galleys rowed by teams of oarsmen provided vessels both for pilgrims and for precious merchandise such as silks and spices. Meanwhile, more bulky cargoes were carried in huge round-ships or cogs, as large as houses. Jacopo de' Barbari's view graphically depicts (with only a little exaggeration) the amazing size of these ships. On the quay stretching in the opposite direction, running eastwards from the two columns, a huge brick granary was erected by the state at the same time as the south wing of the Doge's Palace. Demolished in the Napoleonic period, this imposing hulk of brickwork has since been replaced by a rather seedy garden, leaving a gap-toothed water frontage. Originally the granary stored corn in times of plenty to be released for gradual consumption in lean years, like the biblical barns of Joseph. Visually, its structure complemented the massive block of the Doge's Palace further along the quay.

In the 16th century Venice's particular architectural blend of Byzantine, Gothic and Islamic influences was overlain by a major programme of romanisation, led by the interventions in Piazza San Marco designed by the Florentine sculptor and architect Jacopo Sansovino. Following the Sack of Rome in 1527, Sansovino fled to Venice and two years later was appointed chief architect to the Procurators of St Mark's. His three buildings in the Piazzetta opposite the Doge's Palace created a hierarchy of Roman-style buildings. Using the classical orders of architecture and a gradation of materials, Sansovino articulated a build-up of importance from the old granaries on the waterfront via his Zecca, or Mint, begun in 1536, to the Library begun in 1537, and the Loggetta at the foot of the Campanile, opposite the main entrance to the Doge's Palace. The key to the understanding of the classical system was the first instalment of Serlio's treatise on architecture, Book IV on the orders, published in 1537. As a centre of printing and publishing, Venice was able to produce treatises that combined text and woodcut illustrations.

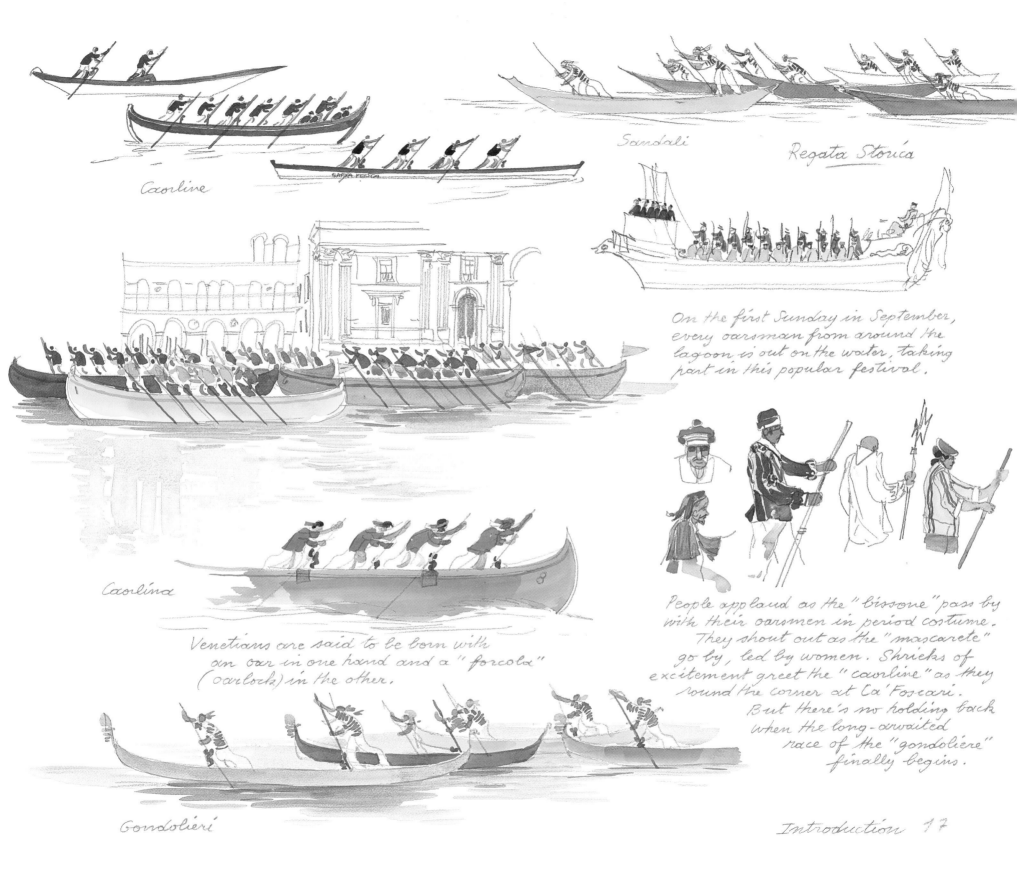

Caorline

Sandali

Regata Storica

On the first Sunday in September, every oarsman from around the lagoon is out on the water, taking part in this popular festival.

Caorlina

Venetians are said to be born with an oar in one hand and a "forcola" (oarlock) in the other.

People applaud as the "bissone" pass by with their oarsmen in period costume. They shout out as the "mascarete" go by, led by women. Shrieks of excitement greet the "caorline" as they round the corner at Ca' Foscari. But there's no holding back when the long-awaited race of the "gondoliere" finally begins.

Gondolieri

The unfolding of these three buildings corresponds closely with the sequence of orders in Serlio's publication. The Zecca was built on roughened Istrian stone, with simple rustication on the ground floor, where a row of cheese-shops was incorporated; a rusticated Doric order on the *piano nobile*, or first floor, marked the position of the gold smelter. (The third storey, added in the 1550s, was not part of the original design.) The Library, faced in richly carved Istrian stone, uses a more refined and decorative form of the Doric order on the ground floor, occupied by an arcade of shops, with a rich Ionic order above at the level of the library reading room. Serlio specifically mentions that the Ionic order was appropriate for scholars. The Loggetta, built of richly coloured marbles, uses the mixture of the Ionic and Corinthian known as the Composite order, the order associated with expressions of triumph. Indeed, the design takes the form of a triple triumphal arch. Since the Loggetta formed the backdrop to processions emerging from the Doge's Palace, it created a triumphal setting for state ceremonial. Sansovino's buildings, accompanied by Serlio's explanation in print of their new classical language, brought to Piazza San Marco a grand imperial Roman style perfectly fitted to the ideals of the so-called 'Myth of Venice' which associated Venice's origins with the flight of the last Romans.

Away from Piazza San Marco the Myth of Venice expressed itself more modestly, for Venice was both an Empire and a Republic. In the more peripheral area the Republican ideals of the simplicity and equality of the first settlers were evoked in a series of projects characterised by simpler forms closely modelled on the local Venetian vernacular, with brick walls and plain, round-headed windows. Several of these projects, including the austere Observant Franciscan church of San Francesco della Vigna, the hospital of the Ca' di Dio and the palace complex for Leonardo Moro at San Gerolemo, were designed by Sansovino himself.

During the last decade of Sansovino's life, the great architect Andrea Palladio, whose career was already well-established on the mainland, began to gain commissions in Venice. His famous treatise, the *Quattro libri dell'architettura*, was published in 1570, the year of Sansovino's death. At this point he had already built a monumental façade for Sansovino's church of San Francesco della Vigna, and had begun a new church for the Benedictine monastery of San Giorgio Maggiore on the island opposite Piazza San Marco. When a great plague hit Venice in 1576, Palladio was commissioned to build a votive church on the island of the Giudecca, dedicated to Il Redentore, the Redeemer, in an attempt to protect the city from further epidemics of plague.

Palladio's churches brought a new classical grandeur to Venice, with imposing giant orders raised on high bases, white luminous interiors and harmonious proportions. Although Palladio had initially found it difficult to compete with Sansovino for patronage, his own architecture was itself to become absorbed into Venetian tradition, so that no future architect could ignore his impact. Most prominently, the Baroque architect Baldassare Longhena incorporated a wealth of Palladian elements into his great Baroque church of Santa Maria della Salute at the mouth of the Grand Canal. This commission, like that of the Redentore, was funded by the state as the result of a vow made during another major episode of plague. In this case the project had the desired effect, for no further epidemic of bubonic plague was ever to afflict Venice again.

The Republic clung on to its established social, religious and political institutions and practices until the very end, but after 1797 the periods of Napoleonic and Austrian domination brought major changes to

The Riva degli Schiavoni
is the place to be at sunset:
from here the Salute seems
engulfed in a blaze of colour
worthy of a Tiepolo painting.

the face and social structure of the city. Innovations included cast-iron bridges, filled-in canals, new streets such as the Strada Nuova, the arrival of the railway and steam paddle-boats. At street level, one must not forget the dramatic impact of 19th-century iron-work. Ruskin hated the triple gas lamps erected on the Riva degli Schiavoni under Austrian rule, yet now these are welcomed as picturesque foreground elements for views of the Bacino. Wrought-iron railings not only made bridges safer in the Austrian period, but also provided rhythmic patterns that could be projected on to paving or wall surfaces by the sun.

In the 19th-century secularisation programme, parish boundaries were reorganised, and many altarpieces were sold, removed to France or shifted from church to church. Following the closure of most monasteries, some of their churches were converted to military or industrial purposes, while others became parish churches. Traditional parish identities were obviously compromised by such radical changes. At this point, street addresses were transferred from parish to *sestiere*: in each of the six sectors, or *sestieri*, of the city, houses were numbered from one to infinity, resulting in the unique numbering system that still teases the visitor to this day. The present painted street numbers on white glossy backgrounds were inaugurated in 1841.

The city is difficult territory for contemporary architects. Although it is the site of one of the world's best-known architecture schools, known as the Istituto Universitario di Architettura di Venezia or IUAV, new buildings in the city are constrained both by the lack of space and by the high degree of protection for the existing historic buildings. Nonetheless, peripheral sites such as the Giudecca and the margins of Cannaregio have gained some exciting new housing projects in recent decades. Other projects have involved the conversion of disused industrial buildings, such as the cotton factory at Santa Marta, now occupied by part of IUAV.

Today Venice faces daunting environmental and social problems. Water and air pollution, rising sea-levels, and the onslaught of mass tourism all threaten the quality of life in the city. Venice must be preserved, both for Venetians and for the international culture that it has so richly endowed. Throughout its existence it has been enriched both financially and culturally by the flow of people from outside. Without visitors it would merely be a small and introverted provincial town with perplexing ecological problems. Its wide horizons must be defended at all costs, but it must remain a living city for Venetians themselves.

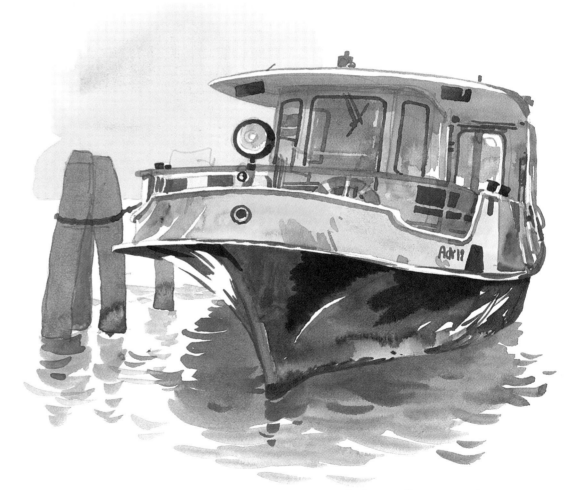

Vaporetti have been part of Venetian life for over a hundred years: this craft is moored to some "bricole", posts which mark navigable water.

Castello

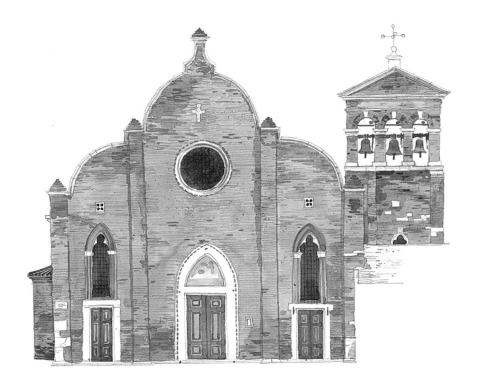

Travellers reaching Venice by sea are greeted first by Castello, at the northeastern tip of the city. Sheltered from the full fury of the Adriatic by long spits of land, this district owes its name, according to the classical historian Livy, to the fortress, now ruined, founded by Antenor the Trojan.

As you wander around Castello's maze of streets, you come out in unexpected places: a dank courtyard overlooked by a Gothic palazzo with exquisite stone lacework; a Renaissance palazzo with an impressive entrance gateway, surmounted by an angel… In the centre of many of these courtyards is a well, bearing the family's coat of arms; often, an external staircase leads invitingly to the upper floors of the building. Colourful washing flaps gently in the breeze, high up on the altana, the typically Venetian roof-terrace. Exquisite fragrances waft from tiny gardens hidden behind high walls.

The stones of Castello tell the story of Venice's earliest inhabitants, who had to work like slaves to drain its marshy lands. They recall a time when this district was the religious centre of the entire lagoon – the church of San Pietro di Castello was for many centuries until 1807 the cathedral of Venice; and the period when the Arsenal was the pride of the Serenissima – when the Arsenal was expanded to occupy the 42 hectares of its present site, several monasteries were swept aside in the process. They evoke the beauty of the five religious centres long gone to make way for the Giardini. Since 1895, these public gardens, the largest in Venice, have been the setting for the pavilions of the art Biennale. It was an important moment for connoisseurs of modern art when, in 1948, Peggy Guggenheim made her entrance with her remarkable collection of works by Pollock, Gorky and Rothko.

While Castello, once the point of entry for travellers, may now seem to be on the the city's margin, it is still perhaps the most working-class and authentic district of Venice. Life centres around the recently restored Via Garibaldi, where there are plenty of cafés, restaurants with terraces, shops, and stalls overflowing with fish, fruit and vegetables. In the midst of all this coming and going, people greet each other, chat, mingle, make appointments. Dedicated anglers gather around the Arsenal docks.

Overshadowing everything are the looming hulls of the Mediterranean cruise-vessels, gigantic floating cities taller than the church bell-towers, stealing the sunlight and blocking the view. At last, when these ships set sail, life regains its natural tempo and the anglers take up their rods once again.

The gothic façade of
San Giovanni in Bragora
with its pierced stone bell-tower,
a feature typical
of Venice.

The Arsenal was once
the world's largest shipyard.
In its heyday during the
14th century, its 16,000
workmen could build a
galley in a single day. It
was a veritable assembly
line, without which Venice
could never have conquered
the world. Huge, ancient
lions (taken from the Greeks
in the Morea) guard the
monumental entrance.

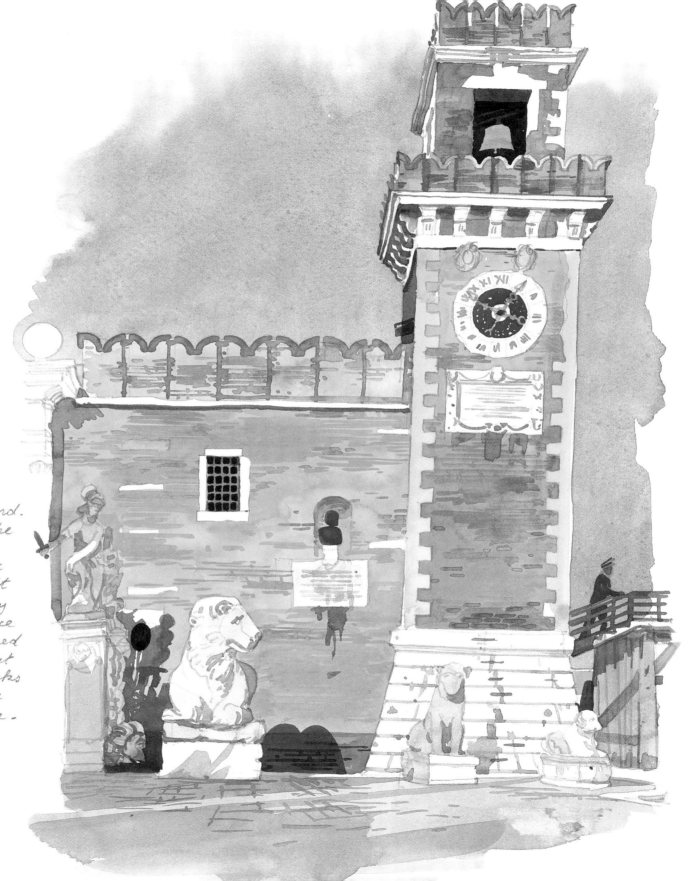

The island of San Pietro di Castello
is one of the last districts still inhabited
by "real" Venetians. The fishing tackle
strung up around the cloister walls may have
inspired the creator of the wood-and-rope throne
displayed in the   entrance of the 2003
                Biennale nearby.

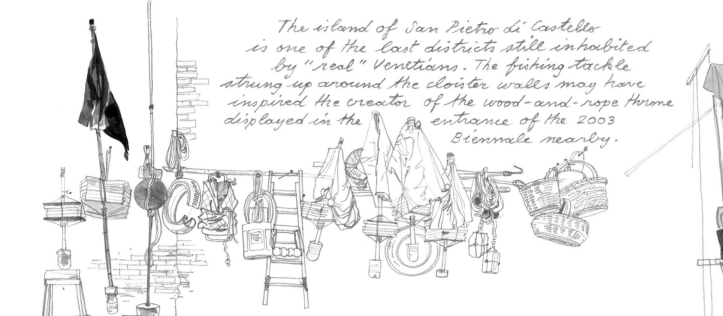

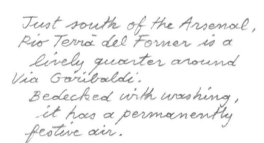

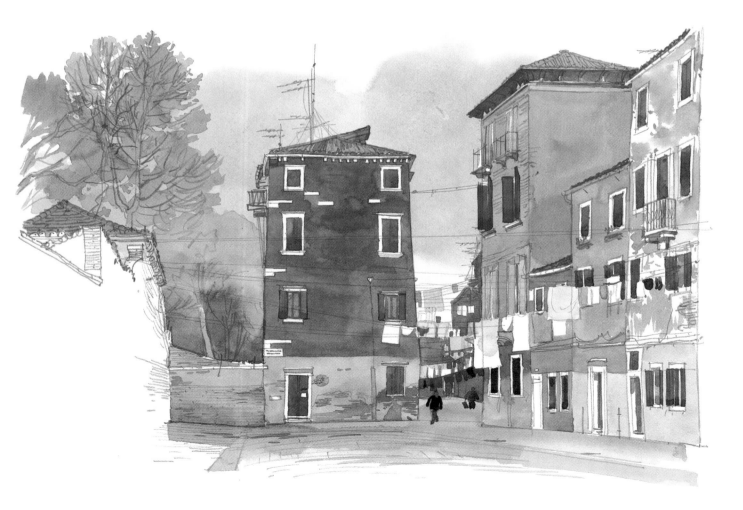

Just south of the Arsenal,
Rio Terrà del Forner is a
lively quarter around
Via Garibaldi.
Bedecked with washing,
it has a permanently
festive air.

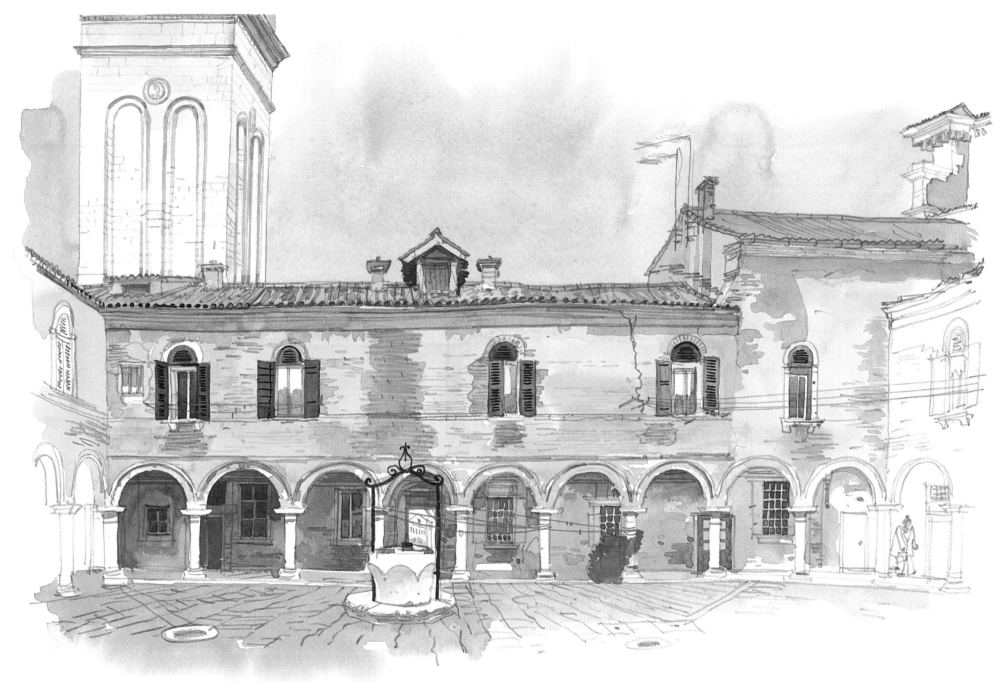

The ancient cloister of the former
patriarchal palace of San Pietro di Castello has
retained its dignity. The central well, the
elegant arcades and the arched window-surrounds
all echo the brilliant white of the campanile
built at the end of the 15th century by
Mauro Codussi. This is the only
bell-tower in Venice entirely faced with
Istrian stone.

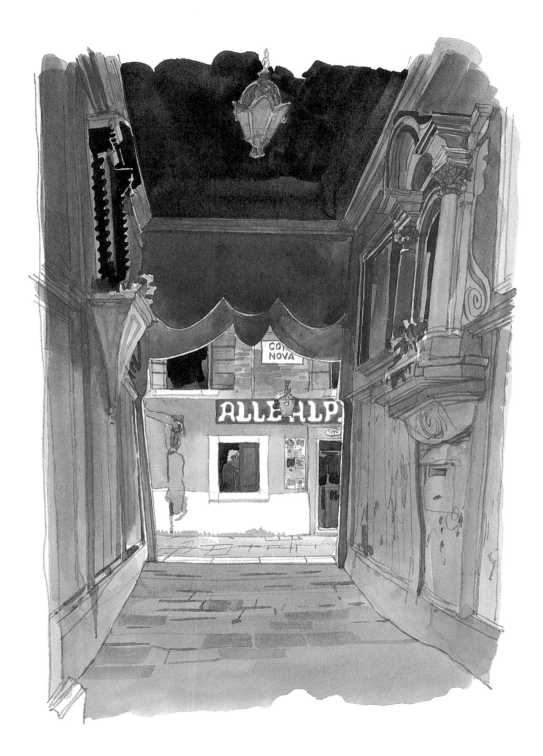

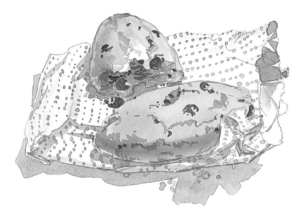

Passagio della Corte Nuova.
Fresh flowers appear every
morning at the foot of this
miraculous statue of the Virgin,
an expression of thanks for the
end of the great plague in 1630.
Below it lies a pink flagstone
laid in memory of a youth who
was stabbed to death by his
jealous rival — it is considered
bad luck to walk on it. Those who
manage to get through this pas-
sageway alive will find sustenance
in the Café Alle Alpi, with a glass
of wine and some "zaletti",
biscuits made of yellow flour
and raisins, a traditional
favourite of hungry sailors.

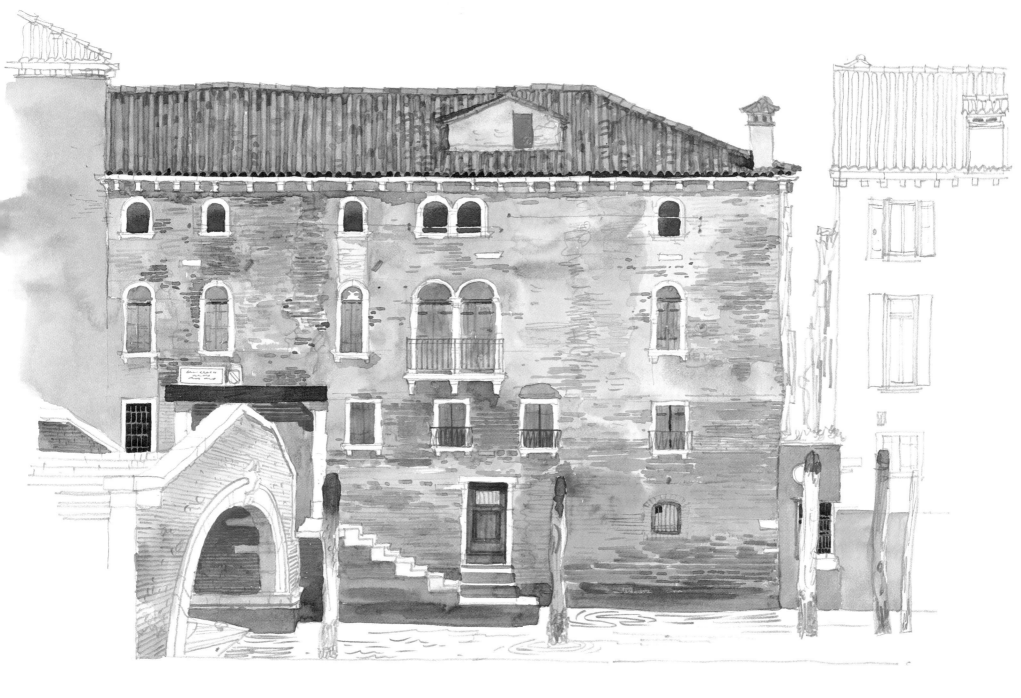

Behind its 16th-century façade overlooking
Rio Sant'Agostin was formerly housed one of the famous
"scuole", the charitable-cum-cultural organisations
indispensable to the economy of the city's "quartiere".

Castello 25

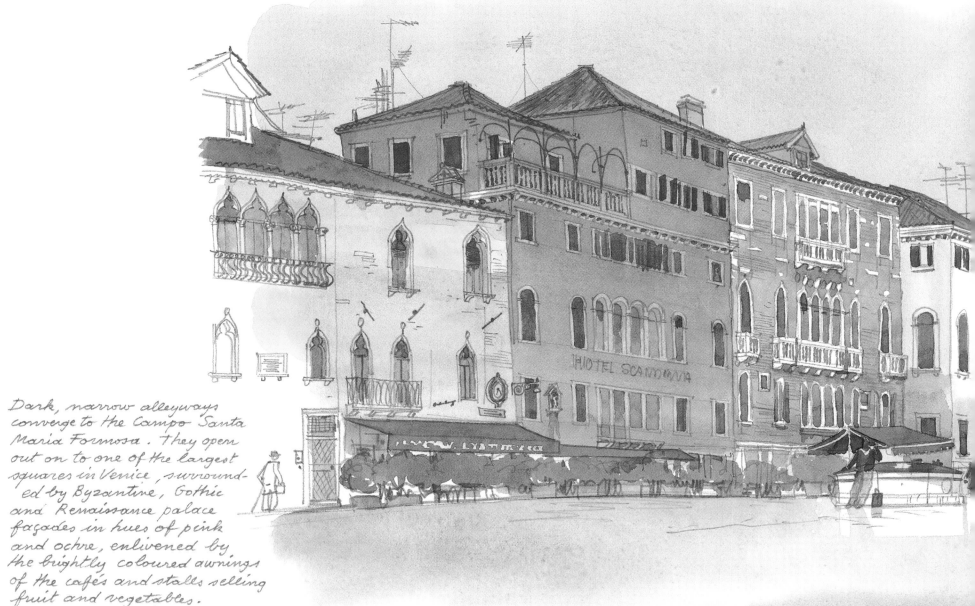

Dark, narrow alleyways
converge to the Campo Santa
Maria Formosa. They open
out on to one of the largest
squares in Venice, surrounded by Byzantine, Gothic
and Renaissance palace
façades in hues of pink
and ochre, enlivened by
the brightly coloured awnings
of the cafés and stalls selling
fruit and vegetables.
In the middle is the church, designed by
Mauro Codussi, looking as if it's been there for ever.
Every year on 2 February, homage is paid to the Virgin,
in memory of the young women who were threatened
with abduction by pirates in the year 946. A boat procession
of great pomp and ceremony used to take place, at the end
of which the Doge would give a dowry to twelve pure and chaste
young women known as the "Marie".

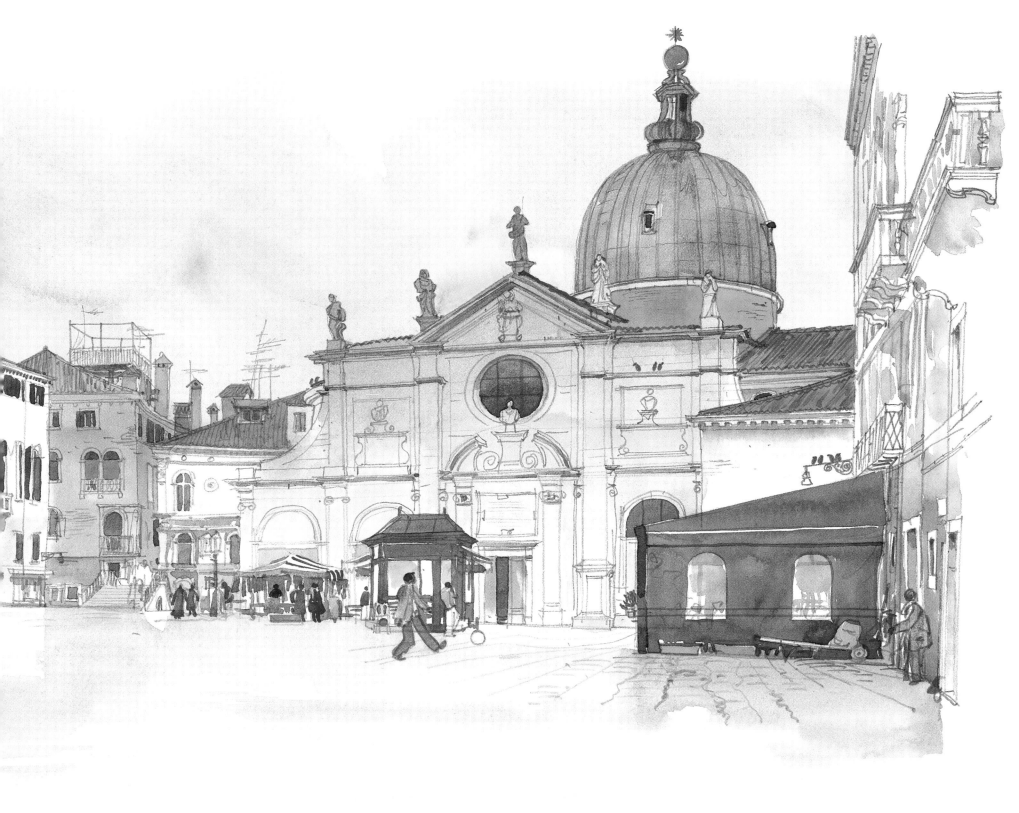

Castello 27

The church of Santi Giovanni e Paolo

This, Venice's biggest church, was the Doges' "pantheon":
all their funeral ceremonies took place here.
Impressive rows of funerary monuments line the nave,
a reminder of the greatness of these elected rulers.
Dedicated also to the "procuratori" (administrators) and "condottieri"
(generals), these monuments are perhaps the best surviving examples of
the diversity of Venetian sculpture.

In 1971, Igor Stravinsky's
funeral was held here, to the sound of
his own music and orthodox liturgy.
Only Venice is capable of such
ecumenicism.
The maestro's remains were then
transported in a black gondola to
the cemetery of San Michele.

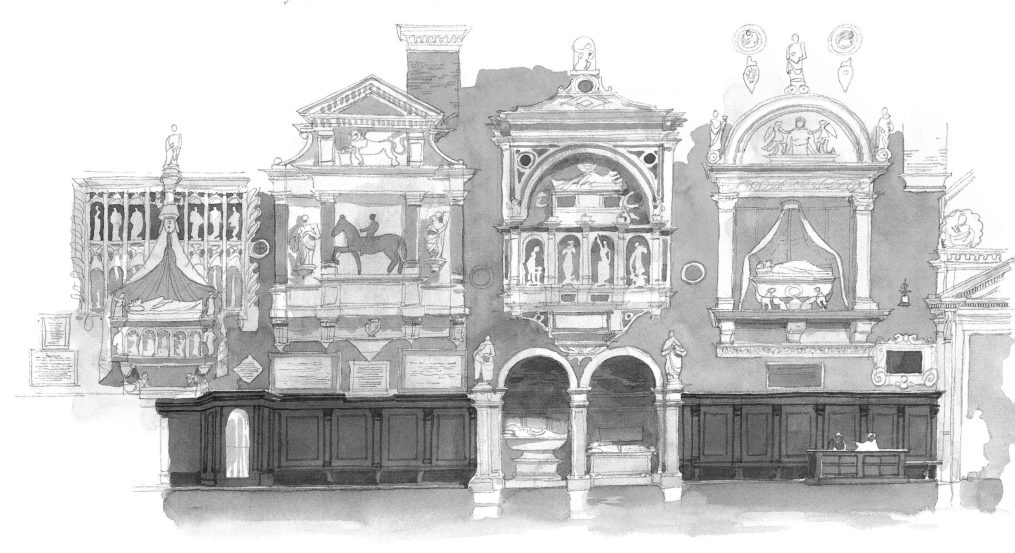

"Acqua alta!"
High water.
The reflections of the houses
along the Calle del Frutariol,
near San Lio, are
distorted as the water rises,
making them look
like skyscrapers.

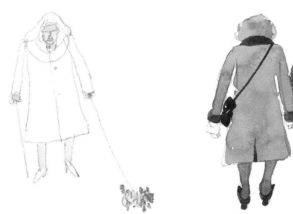

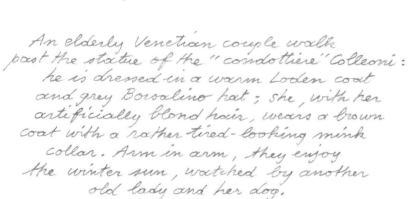

An elderly Venetian couple walk
past the statue of the "condottière" Colleoni:
he is dressed in a warm Loden coat
and grey Borsalino hat; she, with her
artificially blond hair, wears a brown
coat with a rather tired-looking mink
collar. Arm in arm, they enjoy
the winter sun, watched by another
old lady and her dog.

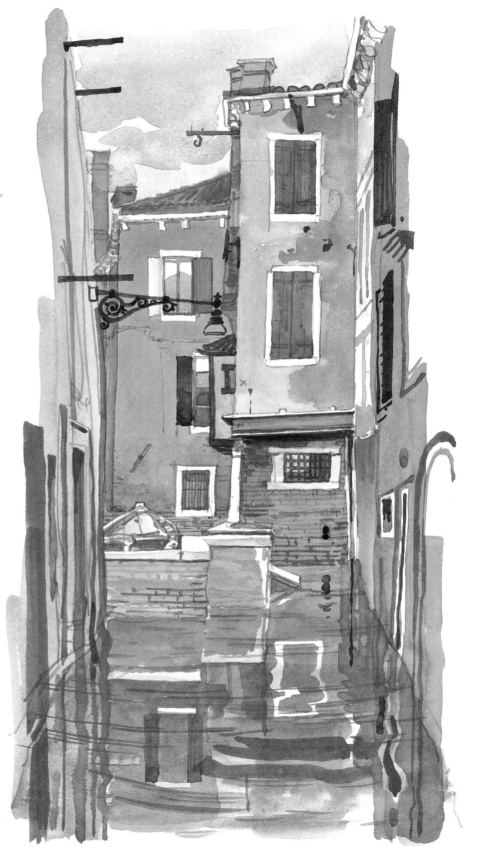

San Marco

In the past, the political and administrative business of Venice was conducted in the buildings around St Mark's Square. The Basilica was the Doge's private chapel before it became Venice's cathedral in 1897, taking the place of San Pietro di Castello. It is the symbol of the city, a meeting of East and West, combining Byzantine domes and mosaics with a Romanesque structure; precious marble lines the floor in the manner of carpets in a mosque. The Doge's Palace, once the seat of government, is now a museum, as are the administrative offices of the Procuratie Nuove, built by Scamozzi and Longhena. The church of San Geminiano, opposite the Basilica, has disappeared to make way for the Neoclassical Ala Napoleonica, built by Giuseppe Soli, while the Procuratie Vecchie now house restaurants and shops.

St Mark's campanile, all 98 metres (nearly 322 feet) of it, towers above everything, as clearly seen in Jacopo De' Barbari's famous panoramic map, dating from 1500. After its dramatic collapse in 1902, an exact replica was built, completed in 1912. From the top, Venice can be seen spreading out into the lagoon, encircled by her crown of islands like a queen on her shining throne. The vast number of bell-towers, about a hundred in all, creates a perspective of vertical lines which define the city. Without them, Venice would be no more than a slight strip of land suspended between sky and sea. To the east, the view stretches across the domes of St Mark's to the Lido and the Adriatic. To the south lie the islands of San Giorgio and the Giudecca, with the church of the Redentore and the Mulino Stucky. To the west, in the foreground, stands La Salute, after which the eye reaches as far as the Marittima port. To the northwest is the Piazzale Roma, where the cars driven across the Ponte della Libertà have to stop, as well as the railway station with the Ponte della Ferrovia, carrying parallel tracks which link the island to the mainland like an umbilical cord. To the northeast, the cypress trees of San Michele, with the chimneys of the Murano glassworks rising up behind, and, further still, Torcello, which, on dank winter days, seems to melt into the snowy mountains beyond.

The entire district, with its sparkling shop windows, its grand hotels, its banks and smart offices, and the Fenice theatre, restored at long last, is centred on the legendary square. San Marco is linked to Dorsoduro by the Accademia bridge and to San Polo by the Rialto bridge, while separating it from Castello is a canal that changes its name four times depending on which church it is passing.

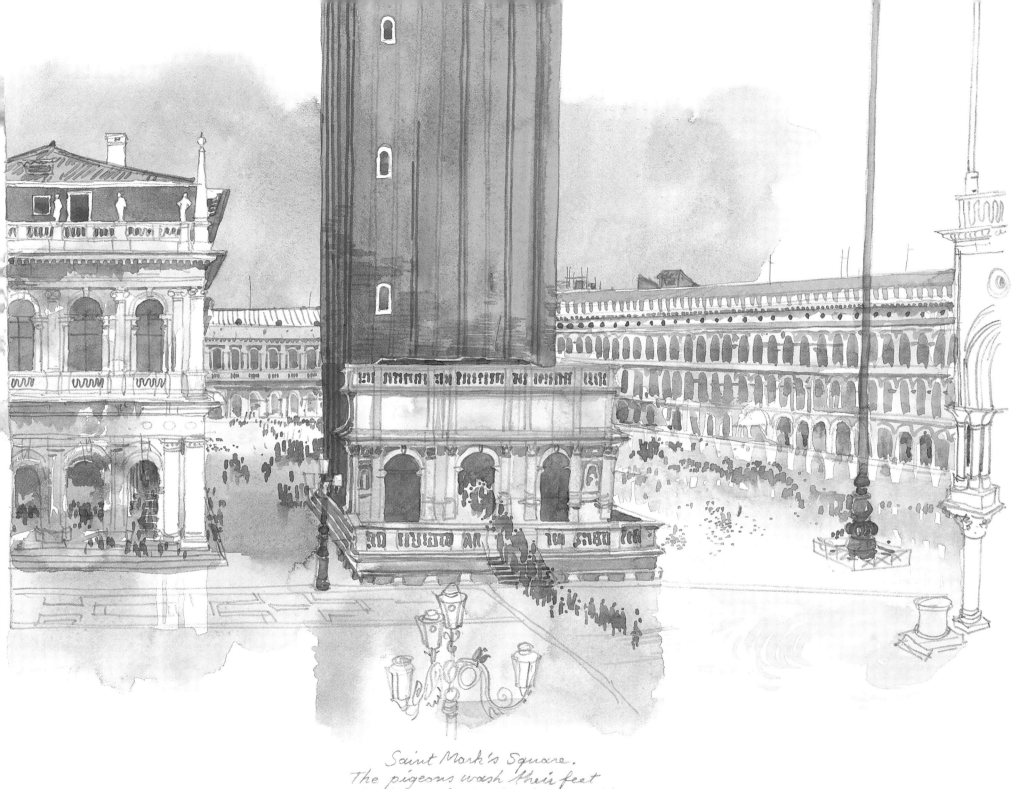

Saint Mark's Square.
The pigeons wash their feet
in front of the Basilica, while
tourists splash happily about—
They can say they've seen
"l'acqua alta".

San Marco 31

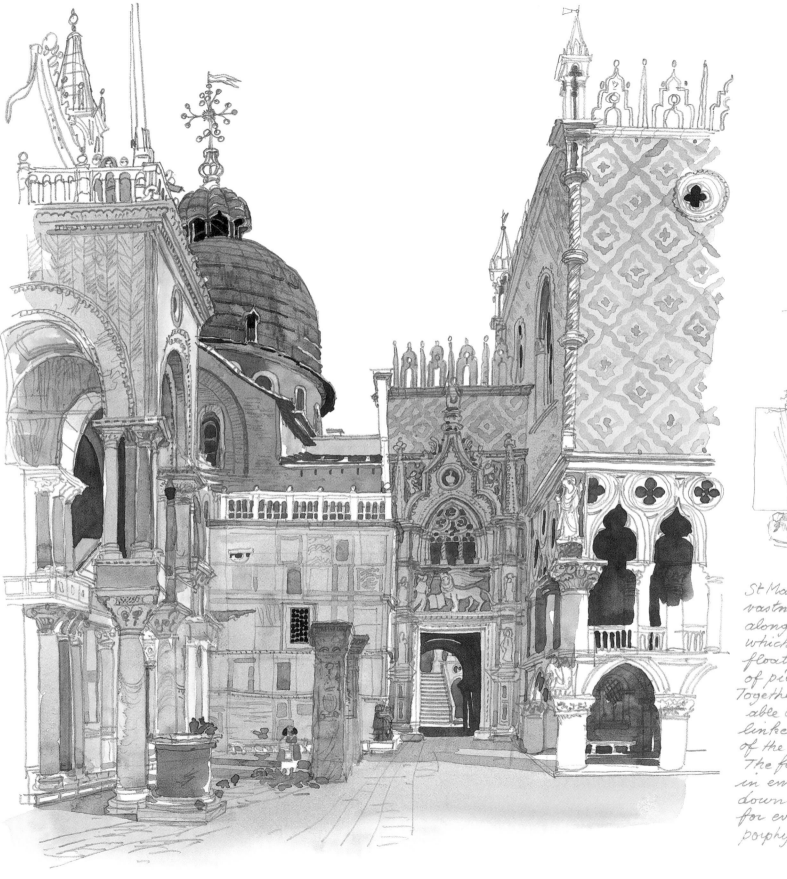

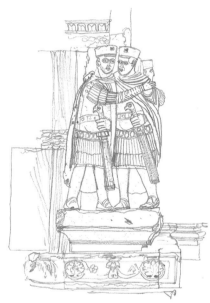

St Mark's Basilica, in all its vastness, is perfectly at ease alongside the Doge's Palace, which itself appears to be floating on fragile arcades of pierced Istrian stone. Together they form a remarkable architectural ensemble, linked by the gothic lacework of the Porta della Carta. The famous Tetrarchs, locked in embrace, glance furtively down at us, imprisoned for ever in the sacred porphyry.

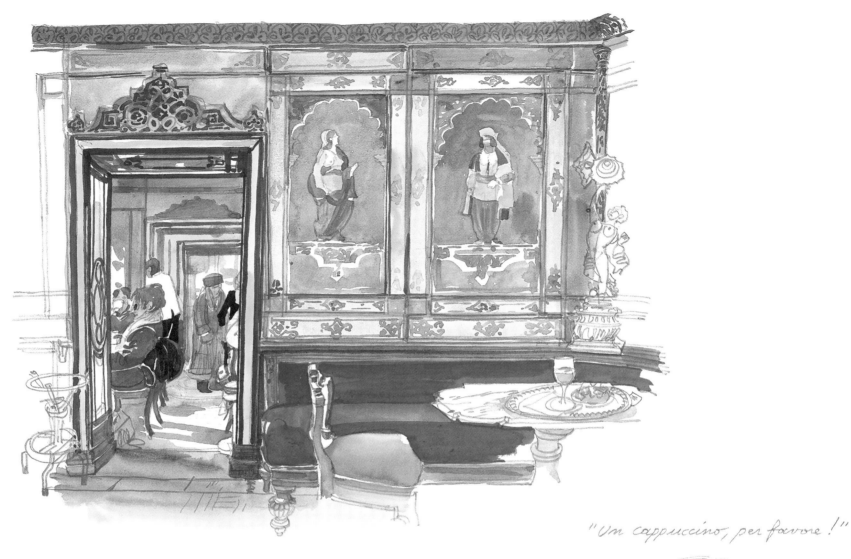

"Un cappuccino, per favore !"

The Café Florian is the perfect place
for admiring St Mark's Square, and for
"being seen". Generations of famous
people have frequented these ornate,
oriental-style tea-rooms for this very purpose :
Antonio Canova, Lord Byron, John Ruskin,
Marcel Proust (while visiting Venice's first Biennale
in 1895), Serge Diaghilev, the choreographer
Serge Lifar, the writer Gabriele d'Annunzio
and his muse, the actress Eleonora Duse ...

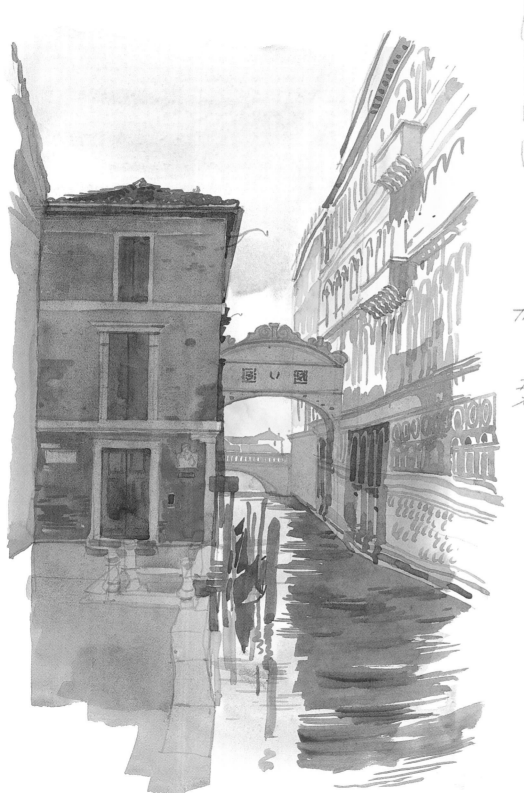

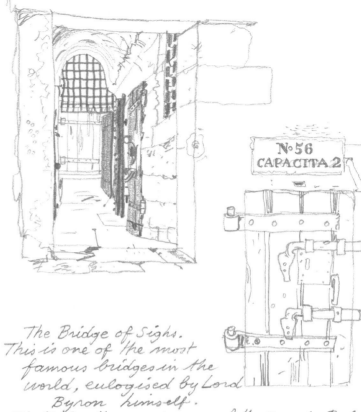

No 56
CAPACITA 2

The Bridge of Sighs.
This is one of the most
famous bridges in the
world, eulogised by Lord
Byron himself.
It links the courtroom of the Doge's Palace
to the prison. The narrow corridor and the
doorway to one of the cells send shivers
up your spine, a reminder of the
near-impossibility of escaping
from here. Casanova, one of the
few who successfully got out,
lowered himself to safety with a rope.

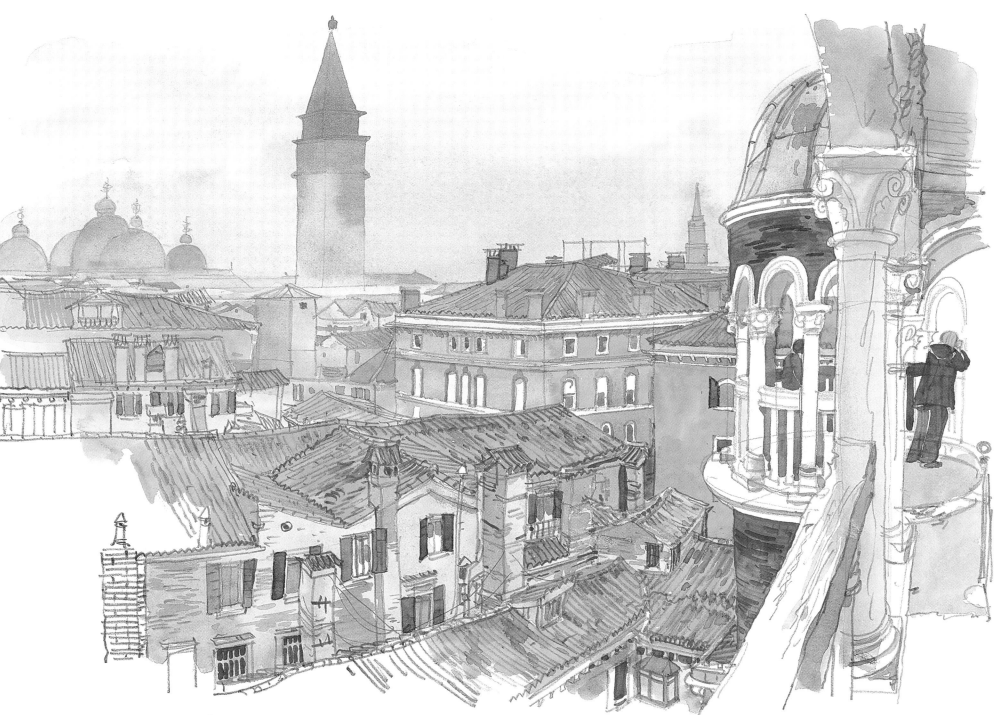

The spiral staircase of
Palazzo Contarini del Bovolo must have
influenced François I when he designed
the Chateau de Blois. From the top of this 15th-century
masterpiece of brick and stone,
St Mark's looks very close indeed.

San Marco 35

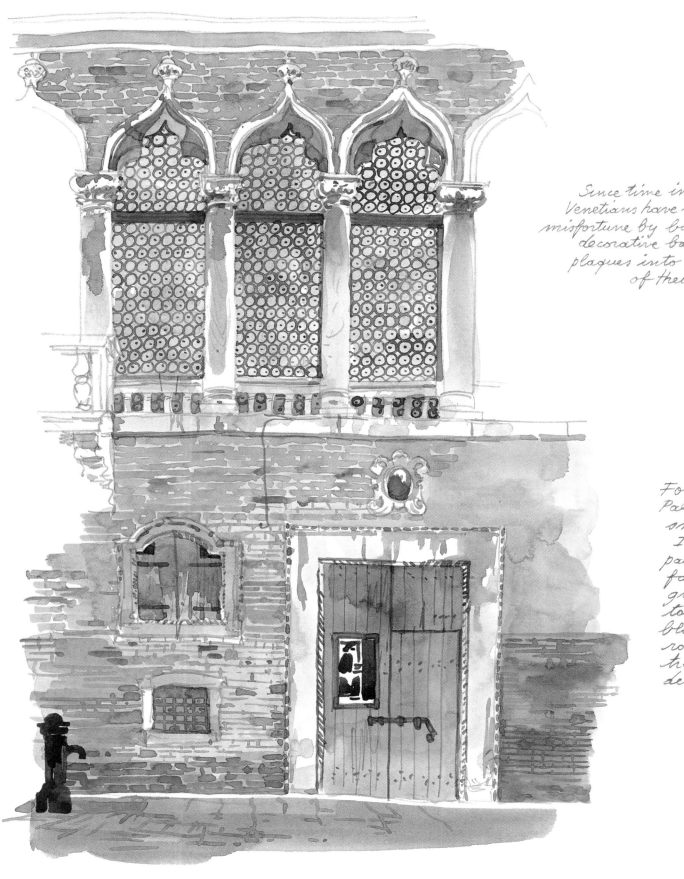

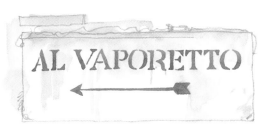

Since time immemorial, Venetians have staved off misfortune by building decorative bas-relief plaques into the walls of their houses.

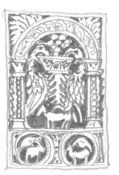

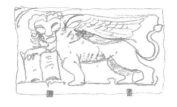

Formerly known as Palazzo Pesaro, Palazzo Fortuny overlooks the small Campo San Beneto. Its time-worn façade is a patchwork of contrasting textures: faded wood, Istrian stone greying in parts, every conceivable tone of brick, enlivened by the bluish hues of the stained-glass roundels fixed with lead. The trefoil windows beautifully demonstrate the genius of 14th-century Venice.

Monet was dazzled by the
golden light as he stood painting
the Grand Canal close to
Palazzo Barbaro, near the Accademia
bridge. The palazzo gateway,
which opens on to the Grand Canal,
is the finest example of
wrought-iron lacework in
Venice.

Bacino Orseolo, the docks
for St Mark's Square.
Awaiting their next passengers,
the gondoliers chat about
the weather, the water level
rising, the water level
falling...

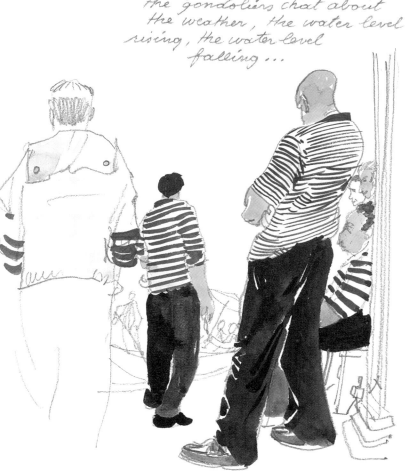
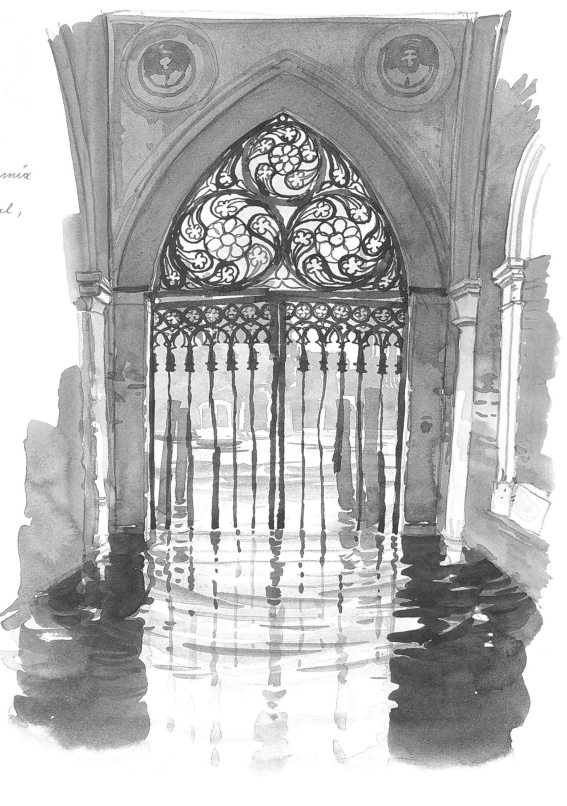

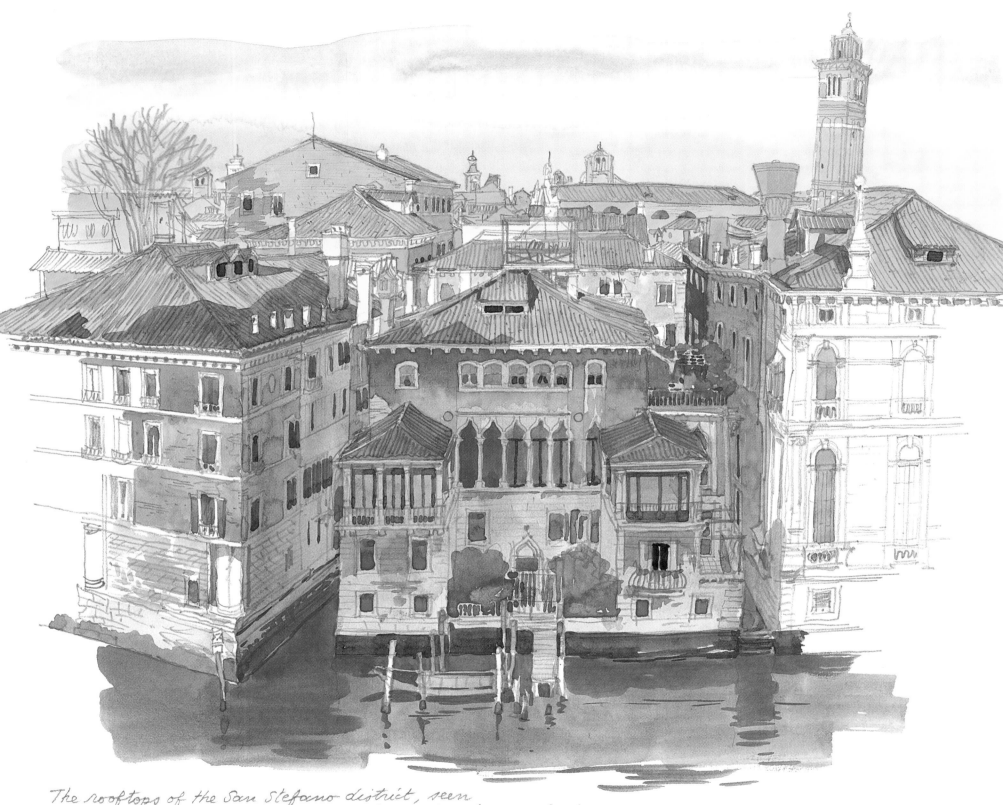

The rooftops of the San Stefano district, seen
from the belvedere of the Palazzo Contarini degli Scrigni
on the opposite side of the Grand Canal.

La Fenice = the phoenix.

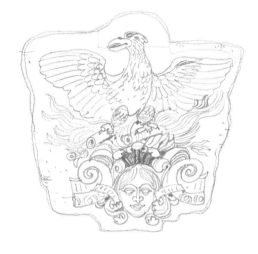

Every year, on 21 November,
a footbridge is built here for
the feast of the Madonna della
Salute, providing an unusual
view of the Gritti Hotel on the
right and the church of Santa
Maria del Giglio ahead on the
left. No true Venetian would
miss the chance to mingle
with the crowd on this floating
bridge, nor to file into the
Salute church, candle in hand.
For it was the Virgin who deliv-
ered Venice from the plague
in 1630. Re-born from its
ashes, the Fenice Theatre rises up
amid the mass of churchgoers.

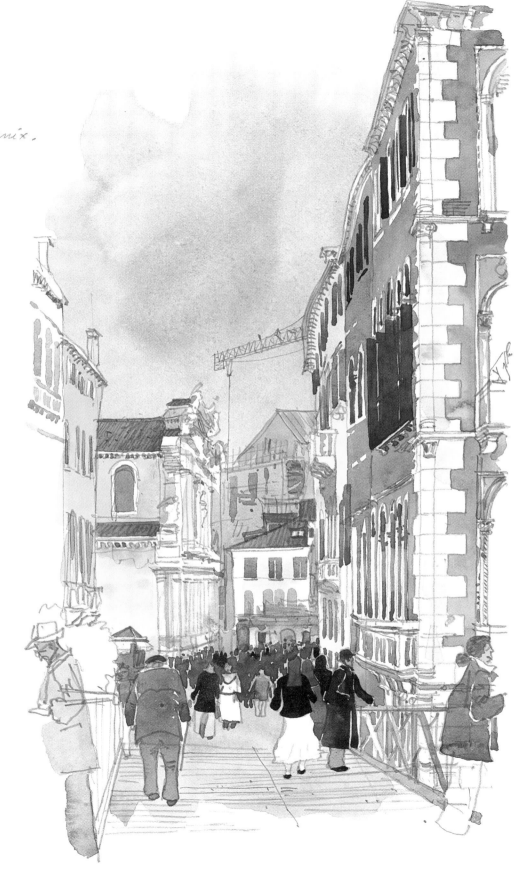

Cannaregio

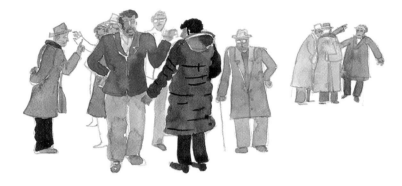

Cannaregio is the largest and most densely populated district of Venice. It is the northernmost extremity of the city, and owes its name to the reeds which grew abundantly on the foreshore and which provided refuge for the first settlers. If Castello's preoccupation was fishing and the sea, agriculture was the main activity of Cannaregio.

Alongside the interminable parallel canals which flow past the churches of the Madonna dell'Orto, della Sensa, della Misericordia and San Gerolamo, are three quaysides, linked by bridges and alleyways at right-angles to the canals, creating a tightly-packed maze of lines. A former canal, adjacent to the Grand Canal and covered over at the end of the 19th century, is now the Strada Nuova, the main artery flowing between the station and the Rialto. The result is a grid of pedestrian and aquatic circulation routes which, back in 1275, Martino da Canal described in the following way: 'Merchandise disperses through this city like water from a spring. Venice rises up out of the sea and water runs off her in every direction. No matter which piazza they may find themselves in, the inhabitants of this island have the choice of returning home on foot or by boat.'

The Cannaregio canal links the northern part of the lagoon to the Grand Canal. It is lined with magnificent private residences, such as Palazzo Savorgnan with its gardens, now open to the public; Palazzo Labia with its sumptuous Tiepolo frescoes; and many others desperately in need of restoration.

The westernmost section of Cannaregio, which borders the Santa Croce district, is a rectangle of land containing Santa Lucia train station, where the long, straight railway lines run parallel to the canals that surround it. Three main sources document the transformation of this area. The first is Lodovico Ughi's 1729 map, the first large-scale planigraph of Venice, which shows how the cultivated fields gradually became gardens. Combatti's 1885 map shows the changes brought about by the construction of the bridge across the lagoon, completed in 1846: the station, the general urbanisation of the district, and the alterations made to many of its buildings – palaces, churches and monasteries alike. Here too, the green spaces are meticulously recorded. Thirdly there are the aerial photographs taken in 1984, which show everything in great detail: the rooftops, streets, canals, gardens and fields. It is only when the city is seen from the sky or from the belltowers that Venice's secrets are unveiled.

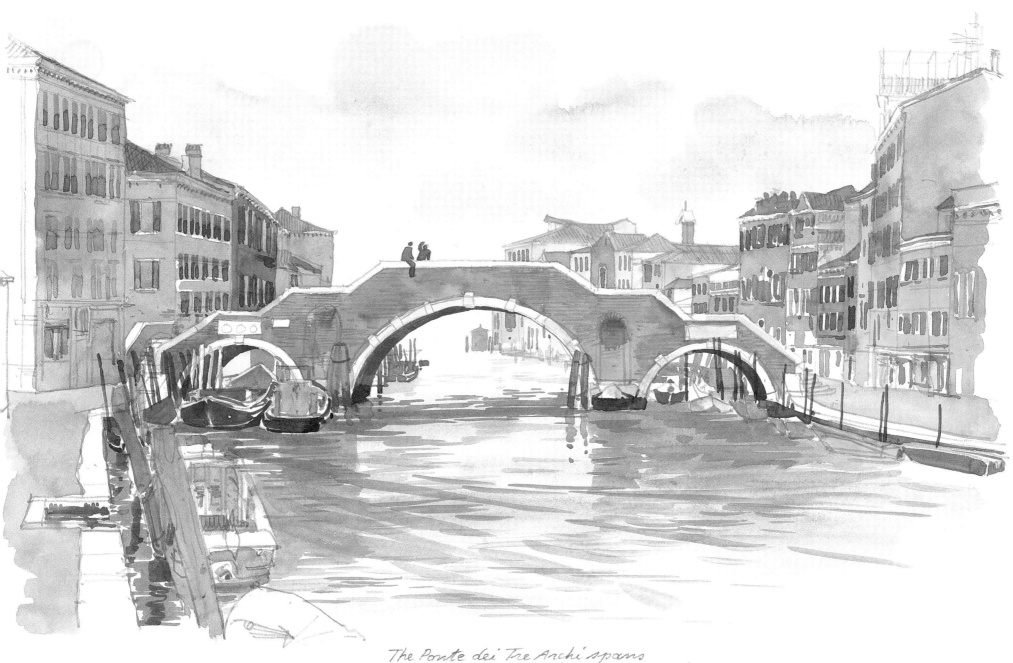

The Ponte dei Tre Archi spans
Cannaregio canal, its three arches
framing the mysterious vastness
of the northern section of
the lagoon.

Cannaregio 41

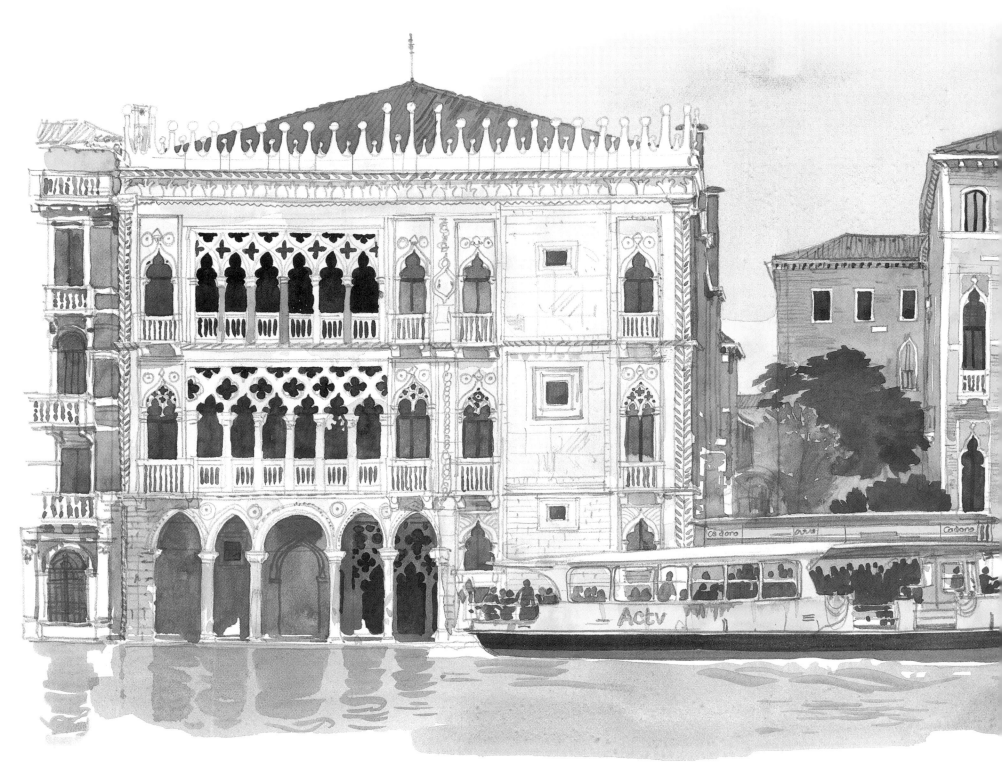

On the Grand Canal, the Ca' d'Oro,
a masterpiece of Venetian Gothic, seems to rise straight up out of the water.

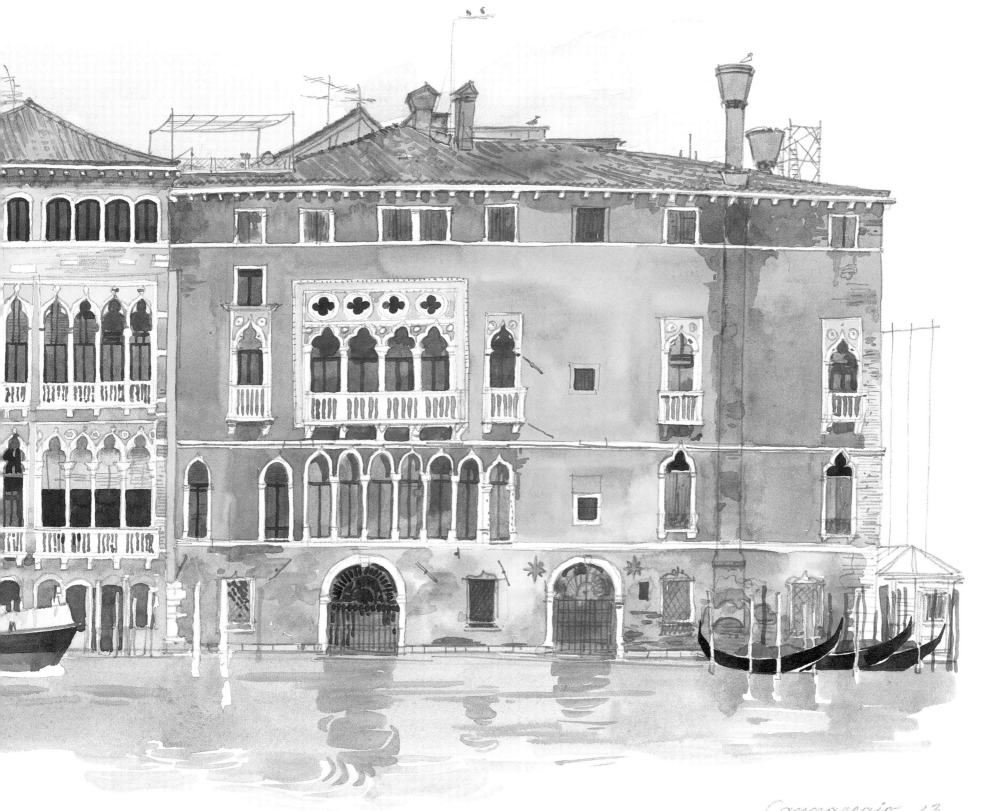

Cannaregio 43

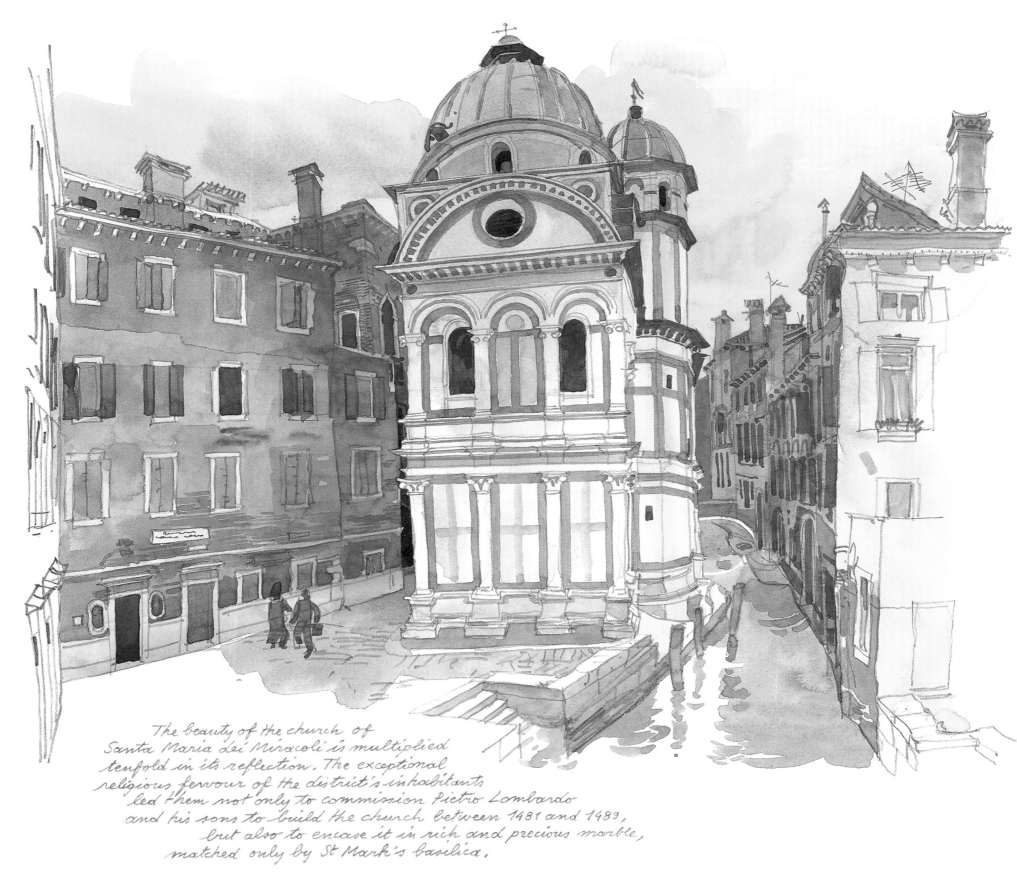

The beauty of the church of
Santa Maria dei Miracoli is multiplied
tenfold in its reflection. The exceptional
religious fervour of the district's inhabitants
led them not only to commission Pietro Lombardo
and his sons to build the church between 1481 and 1489,
but also to encase it in rich and precious marble,
matched only by St Mark's basilica.

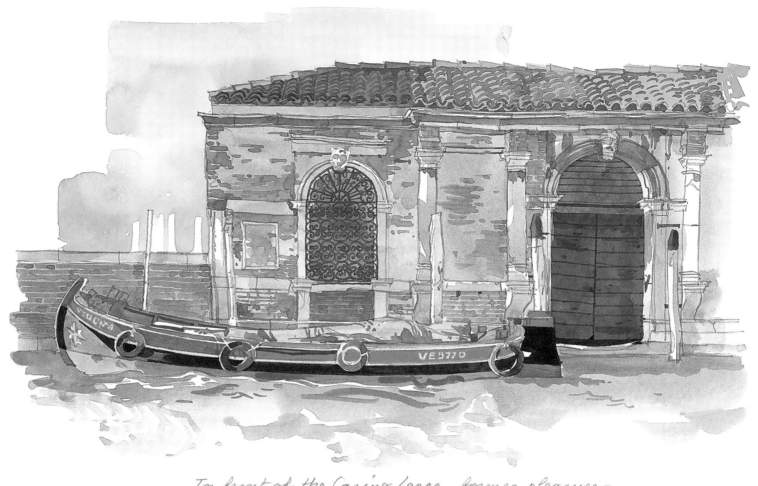

In front of the Casino Lezze, former pleasure-
house, on the Misericordia canal.
A gleaming boat waits patiently, ignorant of the past.
Thankfully there are still many "osterie" (taverns) in this
district, offering "chichetti", those Venetian tapas – a myriad
ways of serving small,
tentacled creatures and other
delicacies, washed down
with a glass of excellent wine.

Cannaregio 45

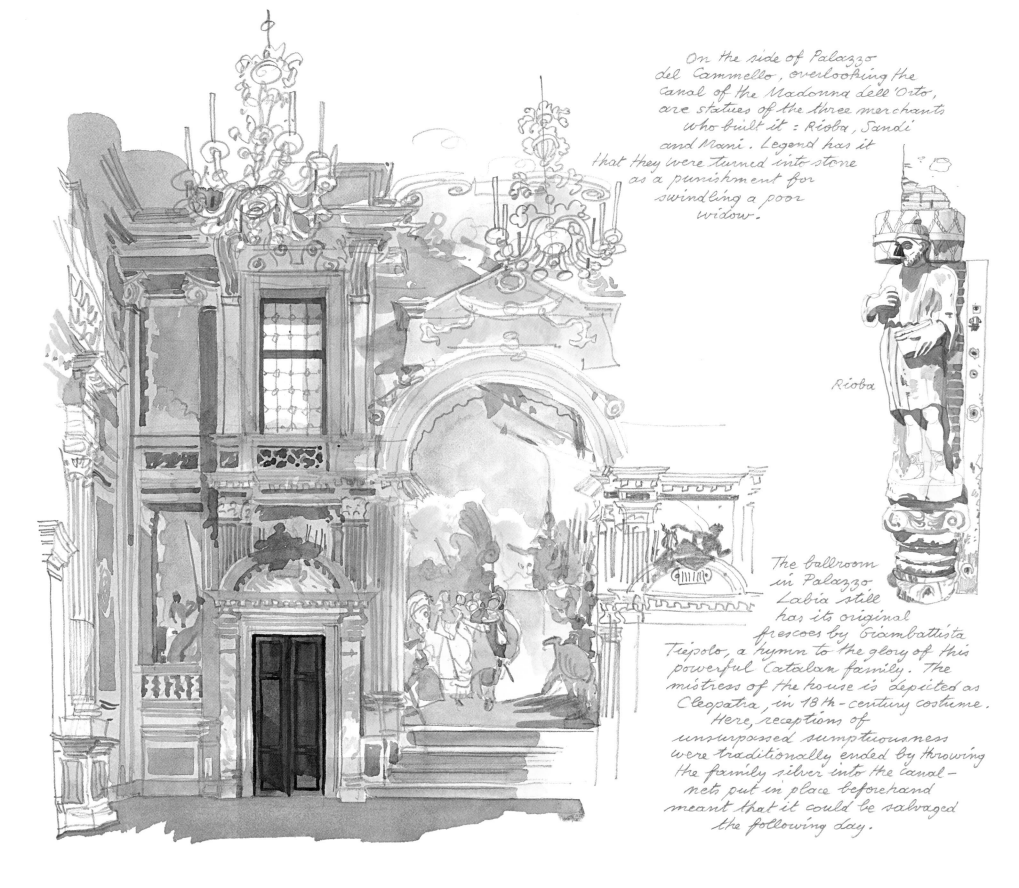

On the side of Palazzo
del Cammello, overlooking the
canal of the Madonna dell'Orto,
are statues of the three merchants
who built it : Rioba, Sandi
and Mani. Legend has it
that they were turned into stone
as a punishment for
swindling a poor
widow.

Rioba

The ballroom
in Palazzo
Labia still
has its original
frescoes by Giambattista
Tiepolo, a hymn to the glory of this
powerful Catalan family. The
mistress of the house is depicted as
Cleopatra, in 18th-century costume.
Here, receptions of
unsurpassed sumptuousness
were traditionally ended by throwing
the family silver into the canal —
nets put in place beforehand
meant that it could be salvaged
the following day.

In the 16th century, the Jews of Venice were relegated to a tiny island in the Cannaregio district, alongside a cannon foundry — "geto" in Venetian. The word came to describe the Jewish quarter; hence "ghetto", applied to the Jewish districts of all Europe's cities. The "Serenissima", the Republic of Venice, granted the Jews this area in recognition of their role as commercial ambassadors for the Republic throughout the world.

The house of Tintoretto

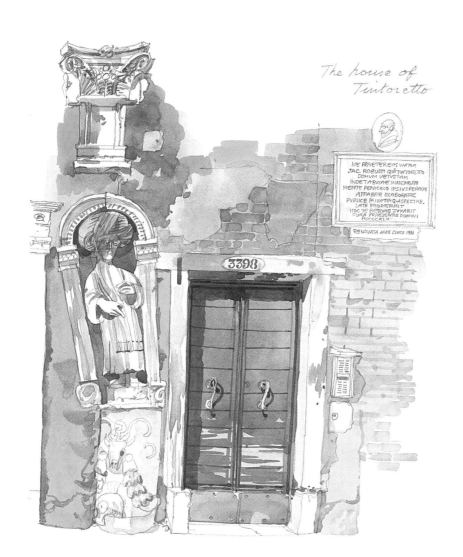

NE PRAETEREAS VIATOR
IAC. ROBVSTI QVI TINTORETTO
DOMVM VETVSTAM
INDETABVNE INNEMORE
MENTE PENICILLO IPSIVS PERACTA
AFFABRE ELABORATAE
PVBLICE PRIVATIM QA SPECTAB.
LATE PRODIERVNT
HOC TE RESCIRE IVVABIT
CVRA PRAESENTIS DOMINI
MDCCCXLII

RENOVATA AERE CIVICO 1891

3398

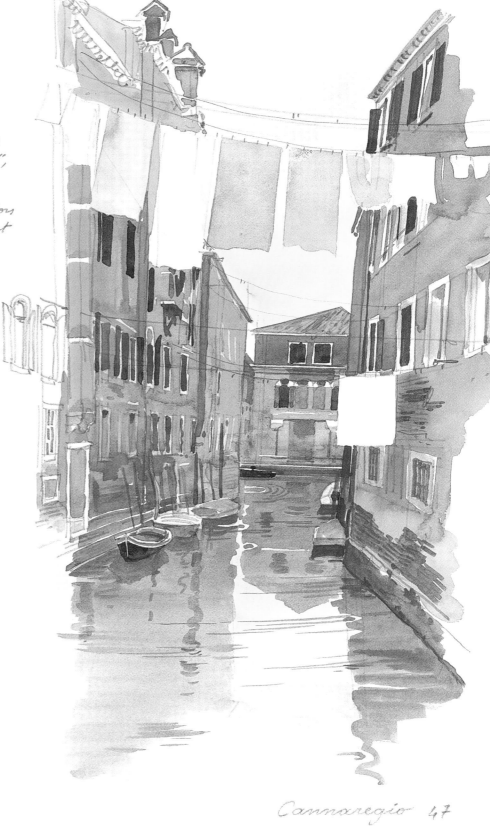

Cannaregio 49

San Polo and Santa Croce

San Polo nestles in the upper loop of the Grand Canal. Although Venice's smallest district, it is perhaps the most important, since the Rialto, as in former times, remains the heart of the city. The atmosphere here is welcoming, working-class and traditional, thanks largely to the continued presence of numerous craftsmen who have refused to move out. This was traditionally the gold-smiths' quarter, as the Ruga degli Orefici, leading northwest from the Rialto bridge, testifies.

Shopping in the Rialto market is a sensual experience, engaging sight, smell and taste. Start by examining the stalls one by one to see what is on offer and to compare prices, and then into the fray! Choose the right moment, around midday, when the perishable goods are marked down – that's when the local magistrates do their shopping as they pour out of the law courts which give right on to the marketplace, which was a crowded, bustling place even five centuries ago. Rich and poor, important people and ordinary people still rub shoulders with an air of civility, albeit one tinged with irony: after all, everybody knows everything about everyone.

You can still find charming spots in San Polo, slightly off the beaten track, linked by old bridges straddling the canals, shady squares with large plane trees, a few overhanging houses…: a village atmosphere in the heart of Venice.

The district of Santa Croce is quite different. On Piazzale Roma, created in the 1930s, the imposing church which gave the area its name has disappeared to make way for cars – these belong to tourists and to Venetians from the mainland who pour into the city every day by the thousand to work. Luckily the cars stop there. The Church of Sant'Andrea has survived this modern development; it is a relic from the past rising up amidst car parks and exhaust pipes. Just cross a bridge and plunge down one of the narrow streets, and straightaway you are engulfed in the expectant atmosphere of the real Venice, steeped in history, refinement, elegance and courtesy. This is an ancient city, but also, as Le Corbusier put it, a city of the future, because of its human scale.

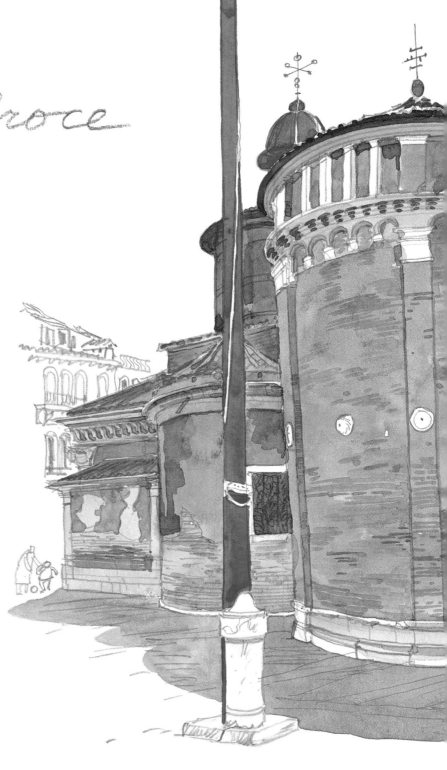

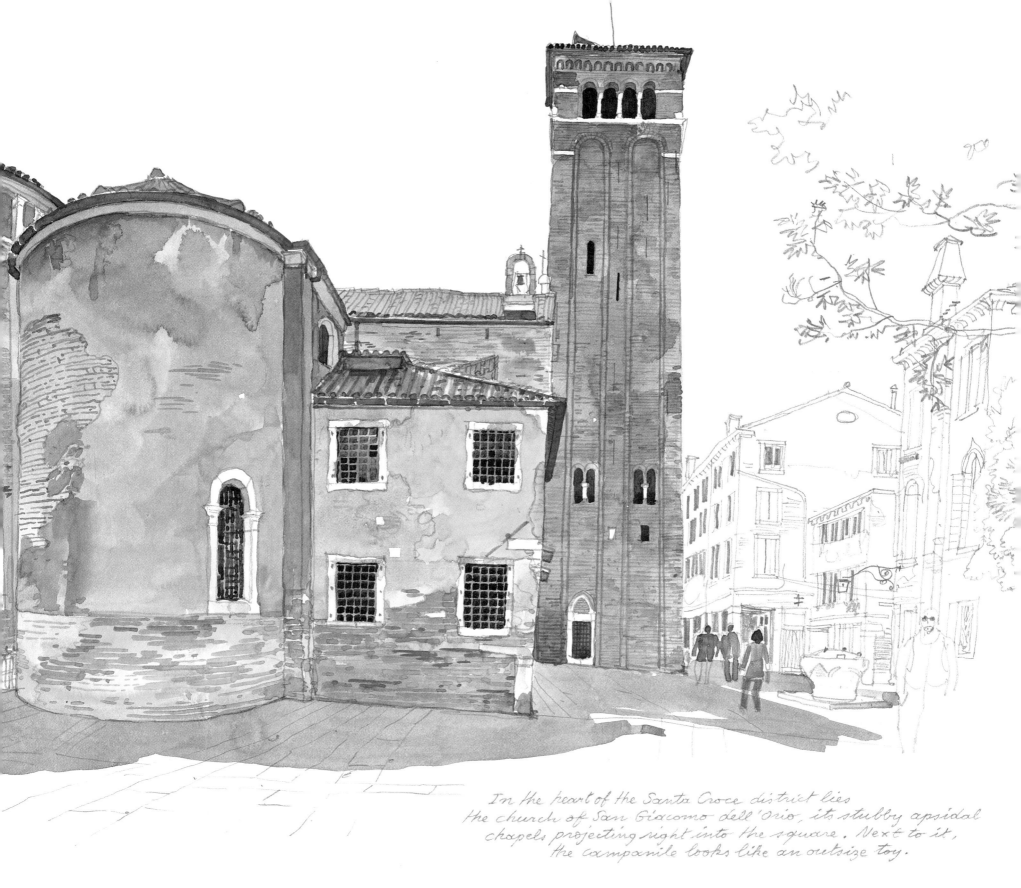

In the heart of the Santa Croce district lies
the church of San Giacomo dell'Orio, its stubby apsidal
chapels projecting right into the square. Next to it,
the campanile looks like an outsize toy.

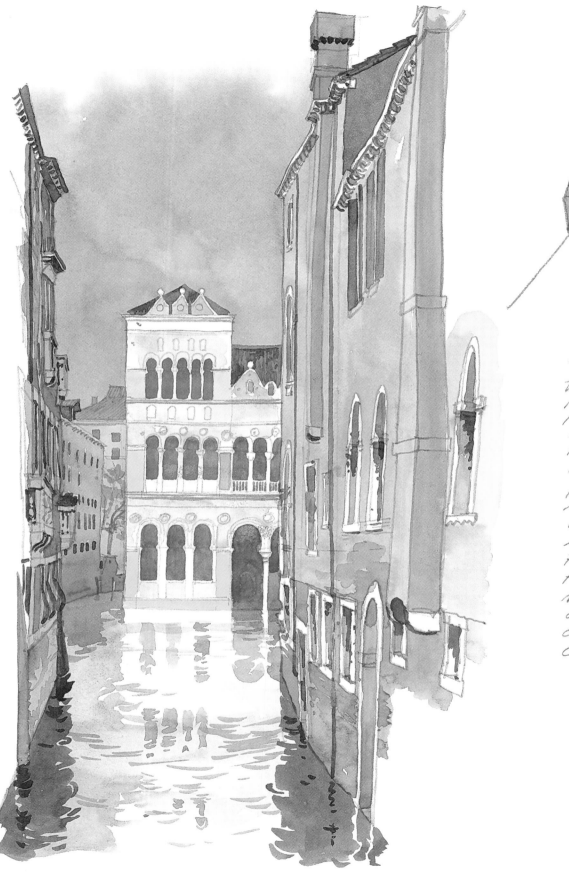

The view from Rio di
San Marcuola, in
Cannaregio.
The reflections on the
Grand Canal take on
a special magic as the water
floods the ground floors of the
palaces, covering the lower
parts of their façades.
The Fondaco dei Turchi is
the sole surviving example
of a Veneto-Byzantine
palace, with a long, luminous façade, a portico, loggia
and corner towers, perhaps
rather over-restored.
From 1261 to 1838, it was
the residence of Turkish
merchants, and still bears
an original plaque forbid-
ding entrance to women and
children.

Far from the hubbub of the Rialto,
waiting silently in side-canals, are
sumptuously decorated gondolas,
    soon to be filled with tourists
    and their reveries.
At their journey's end, they will be met
by a "gancer", a retired gondolier,
who will courteously help them ashore.

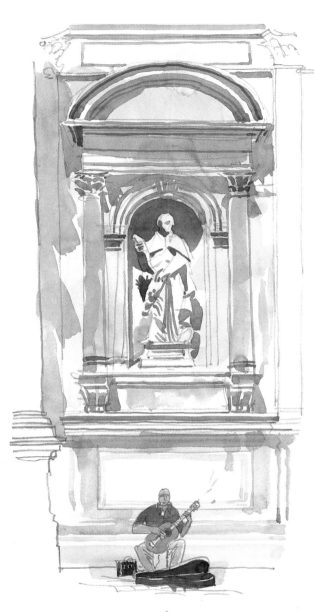

A niche in the façade of the
church of San Rocco.
Since 1485, the church of the
same name as the famous
"scuola" has housed the relics
of Saint Roch of Montpellier,
patron saint of plague
victims.

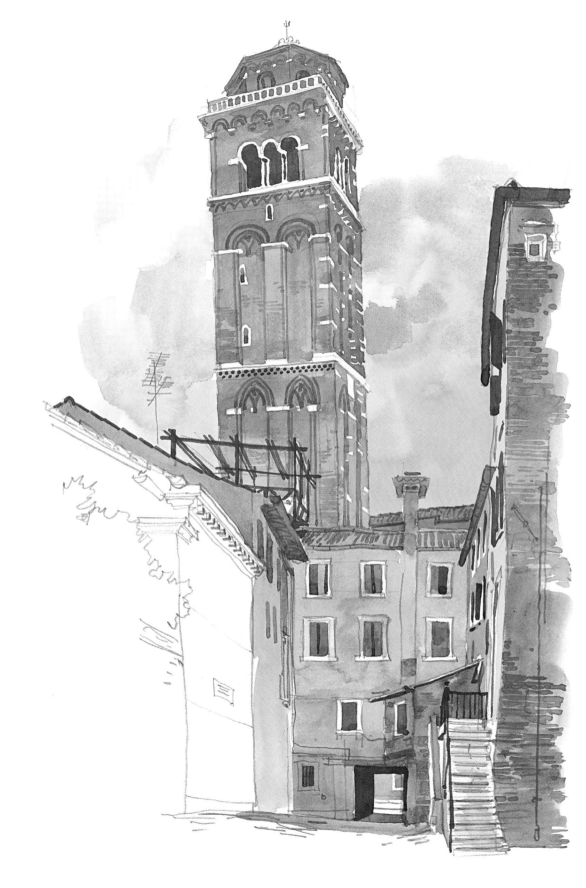

Built between 1361 and 1396,
the campanile of the church of
the Frari looks down over a
small courtyard far below,
with its typical staircase.
From the top, 69 metres
(over 220 feet) up, there is a
magnificent panoramic view
of the Adriatic and the foothills of the Alps.

The rain of a May
morning brings out the
colours of the buildings
in Campo San Cassiano,
just as in a painting by
Francesco Guardi.

The rooftops of the San Cassiano district slowly come to life : one by one,
the bell-tower, chimneys, terraces and cornices take on
their daytime colours.

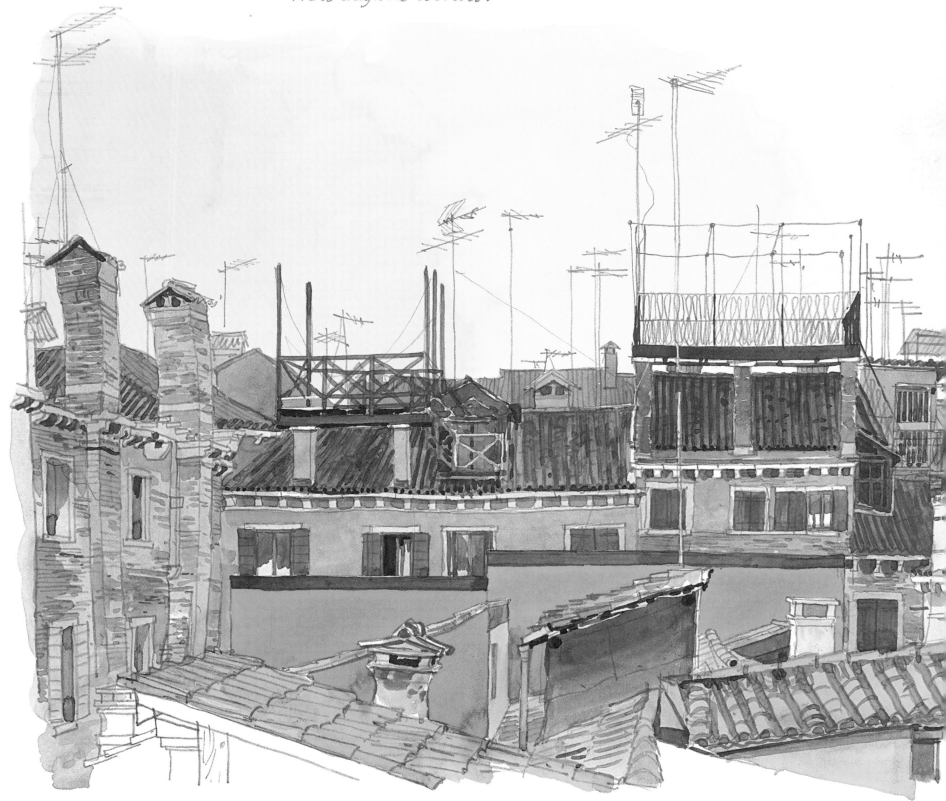

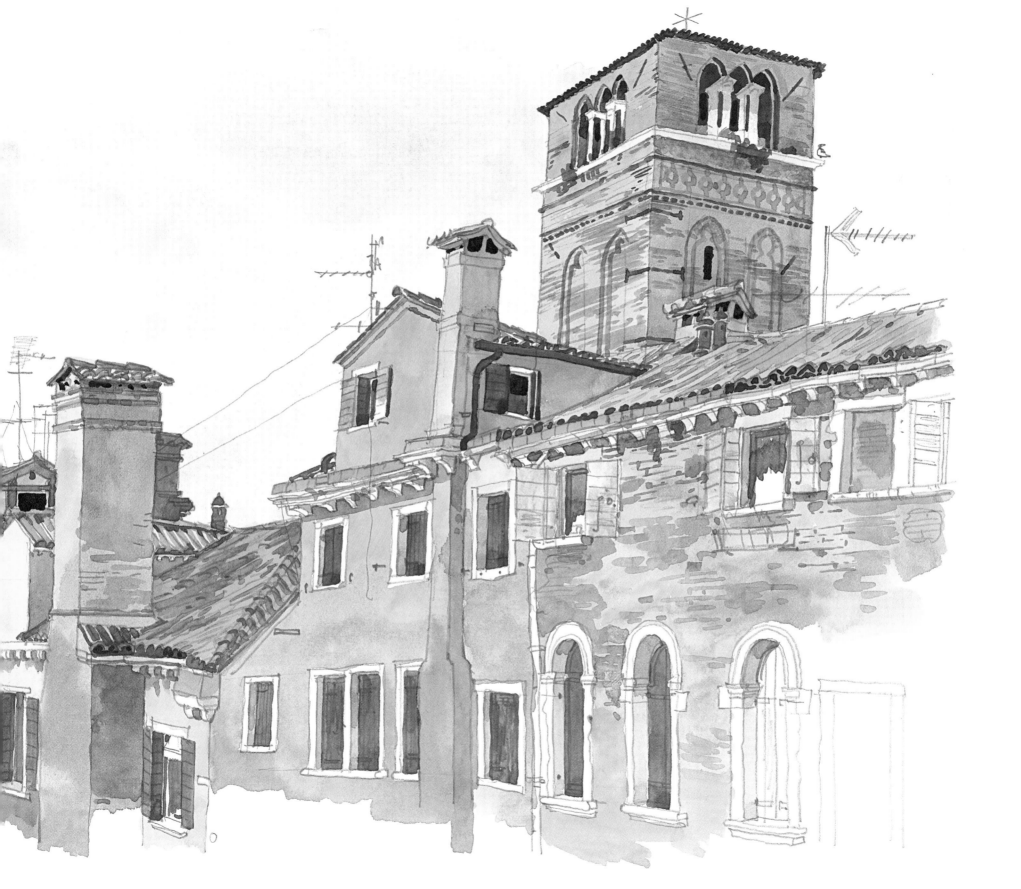

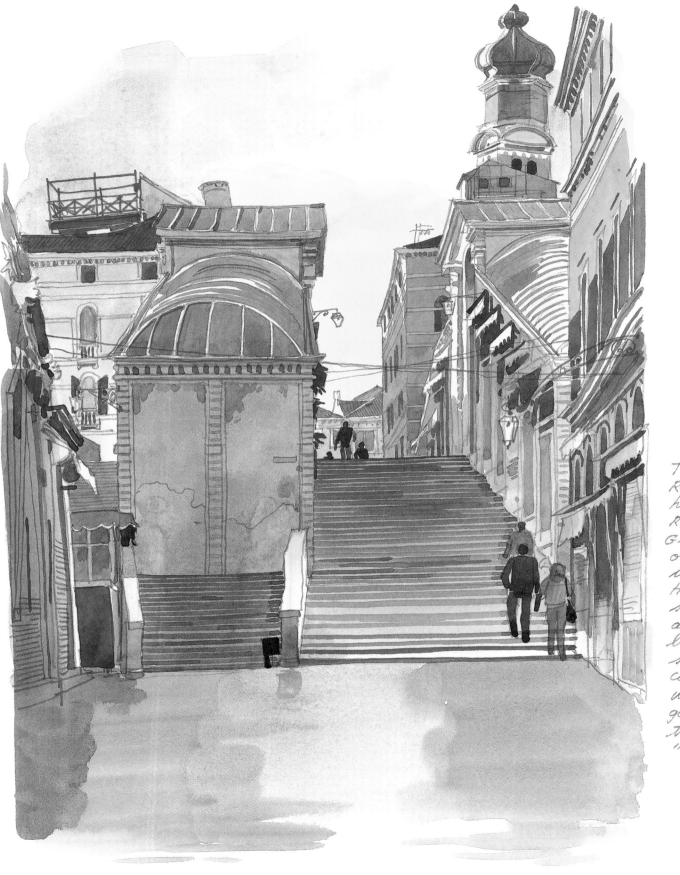

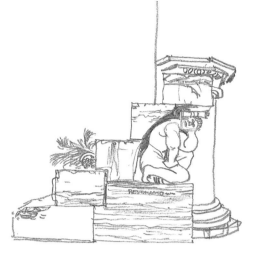

The statue of "il gobo di Rialto" (the Rialto hunchback) has knelt at the foot of the Rialto bridge, in Campo San Giacomo, unchanged for over four centuries. People used to flock here to read the outrageous political satires stuck to his back at dawn each day. The Rialto bridge is not yet awake, but soon this lively district, the commercial heart of Venice, will be overrun with people going about the market and treating themselves to "chichetti".

MACELLERIA

The butchers' shops are in Campo delle Beccarie. The reddish hues of the meat echo the pinkish tones of the fish on sale nearby in Campo della Pescheria.

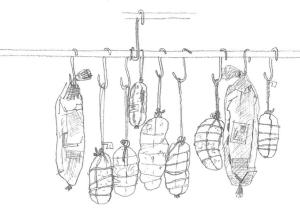

"Antico Dolo", on Calle Ruga Vecchia, is one of the Venetians' favourite "osterie" (taverns) — the spaghetti cooked in cuttlefish ink is the best in town!

Dorsoduro

The district of Dorsoduro is made up of small, compact areas of land resembling a spinal column, hence its name, which means 'hard back'. For a long time it lay uninhabited because it was too exposed to attack from pirates. The area overlooking St Mark's basin, with the Punta della Dogana (Customs' Point) at its tip, is dominated by the superstructure of the church of Santa Maria della Salute. Along the Grand Canal some of the city's most magnificent palazzi flaunt their finery, numerous gardens hidden amongst them overlooked by terraces perched up high on the rooftops. From these *altane*, typically Venetian roof-terraces, you can see the Grand Canal and St Mark's on one side, the lagoon, Giudecca and the Zattere on the other. Beyond them you can see down into the gardens and kitchen-gardens protected from the north winds.

Dorsoduro is a pleasant district to live in, where everybody knows each other and where there is still a sense of being able to get away from the hordes who visit the Salute, the Peggy Guggenheim Foundation, Ca'Rezzonica and the Accademia. The oldest part of the district is its westerly end, around the Church of San Nicolo dei Mendicoli, which today houses Venice's university.

The Zattere, wide quays which run for two kilometres (over a mile) from the Punta della Dogana to the Porto Marittima, are always lively and full of promenaders, except, of course, in times of *acqua alta* ('high water'). The view, the constantly changing light and the reflections in the water are utterly captivating.

The island of Giudecca, opposite, is also part of Dorsoduro. On cold December afternoons, you can savour a magical stroll in the Capucin gardens beside the church of the Redentore, warmed by the weak rays of the sun which gradually slip into the golden, then purple waters to the south of the lagoon.

It is here that André Suarès' words find their true meaning: 'Venice's architecture is born of light. It is light which provides the architect's palette and gives him his instructions. Just as lace is a material in itself, and not embroidery on top of a frame, so the architecture of Venice is a mirror open to the sky and to the light.'

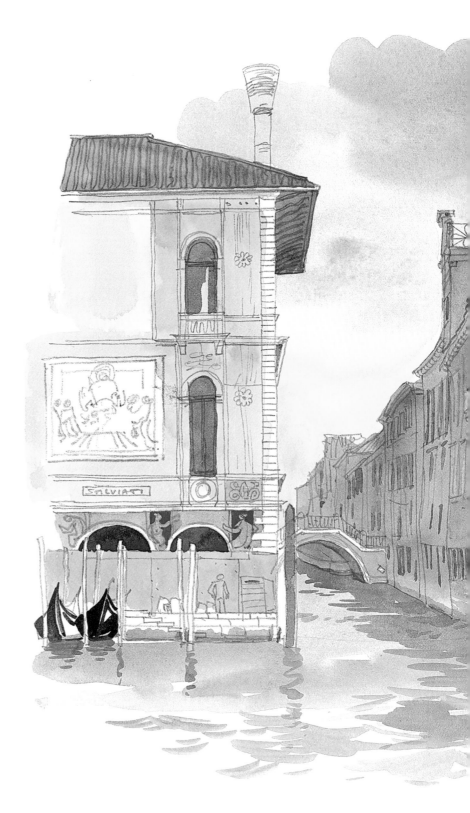

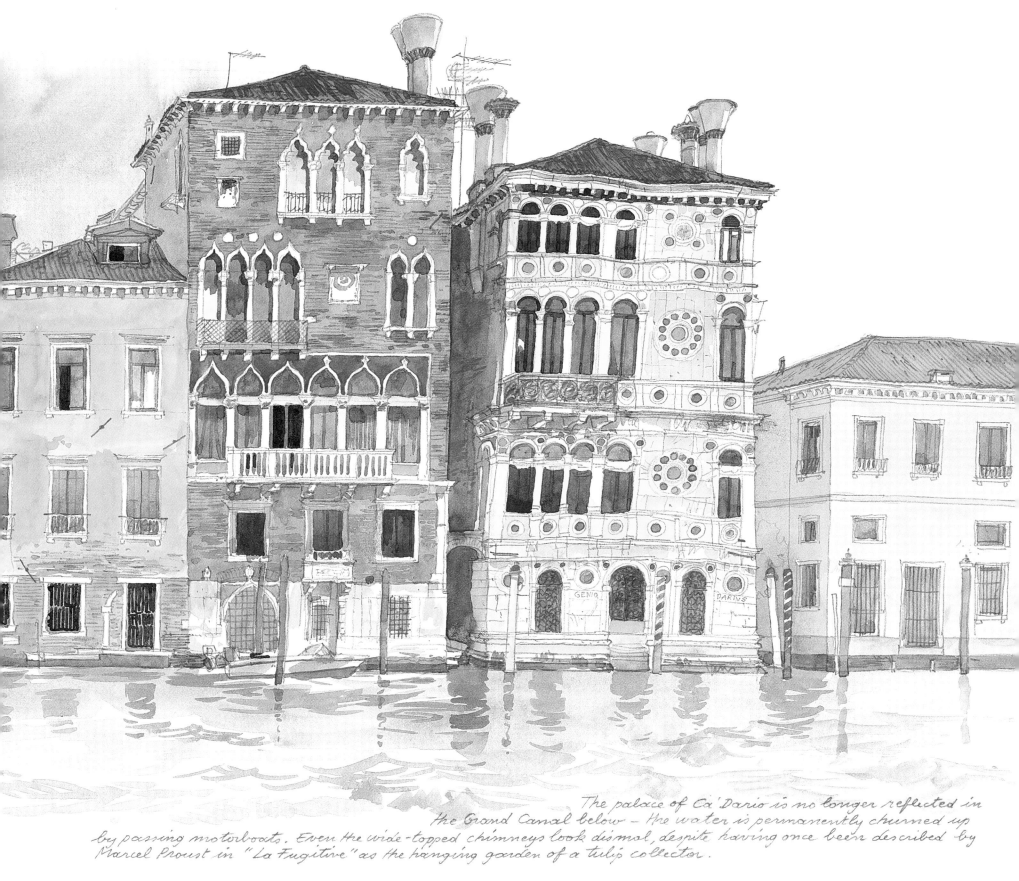

The palace of Ca' Dario is no longer reflected in
the Grand Canal below – the water is permanently churned up
by passing motorboats. Even the wide-topped chimneys look dismal, despite having once been described by
Marcel Proust in "La Fugitive" as the hanging garden of a tulip collector.

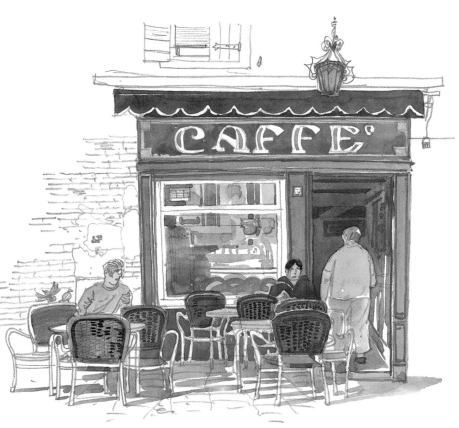

In the old days, people used to gather by the Ponte dei Pugni (the Bridge of Fists) to watch the fights between the inhabitants of San Nicolo and those of the Arsenal. Today, people hurry there to buy fruit and vegetables from the colourful boat of a market-gardener from Sottomarina; together with one other boat in Via Garibaldi, this is all that remains of Venice's floating markets.

Tourists and students from the nearby university vie for the few seats outside the little red café in Campo Santa Margherita.

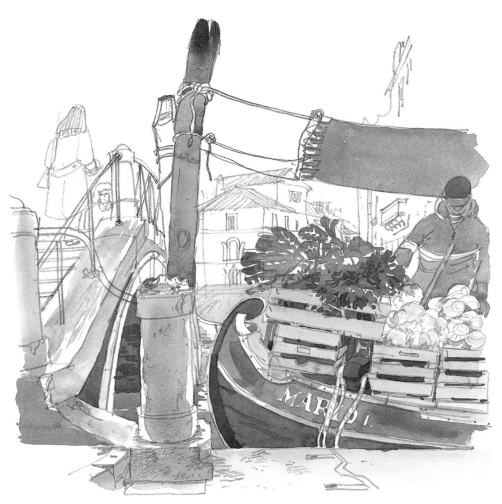

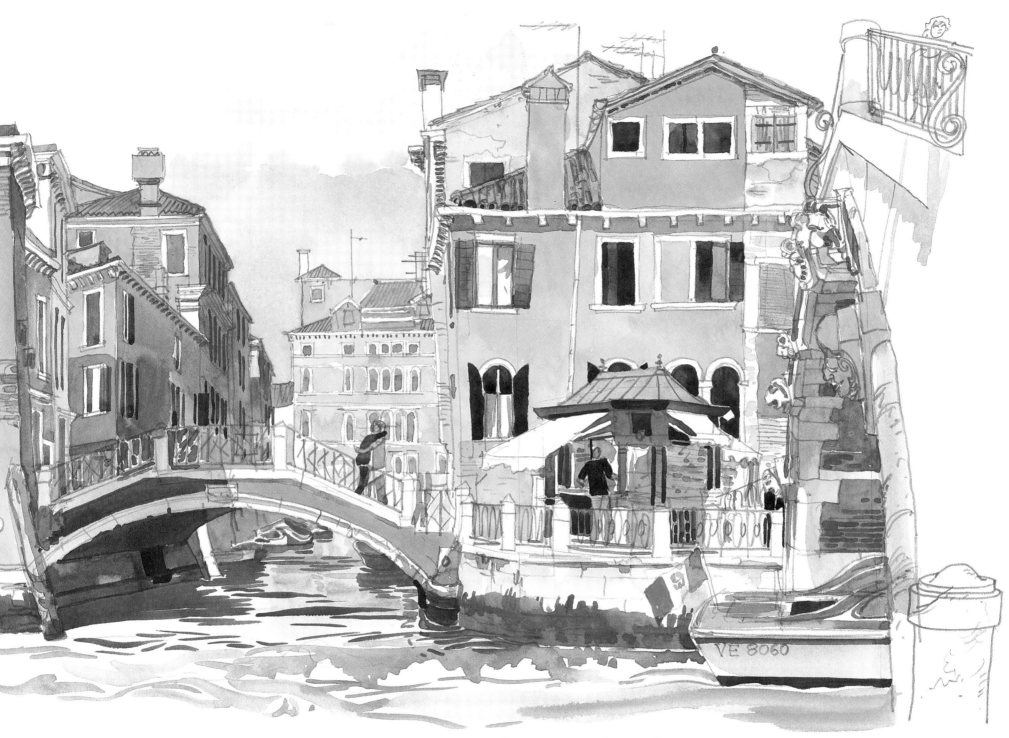

The grotesque masks of the bridge linking Campo San Pantalon
to Campiello Mosca look down mockingly on the lovers passing below.
The Rio Nuovo is always very lively and is a useful shortcut between
the Ca' Foscari and Piazzale Roma, helping to relieve traffic on
the Grand Canal.

Dorsoduro 61

VE 8060

Just in front of the church of
San Trovaso, a "squero", or boatyard;
there were once hundreds in Venice,
and this is one of the last.
It still builds gondolas, magnificent
with their pure, subtly asym-
metrical lines. Venetians
flock from all across
the city to drink at
Ai Schiavi on the
opposite bank.

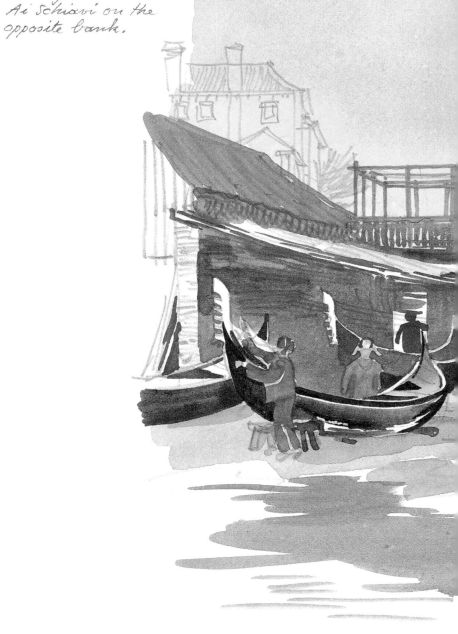

The miniature bell-tower
of San Barnaba disappears in the
January mist. The gigantic white pillars
of the neoclassical façade bear down
on two minute shops at its feet.

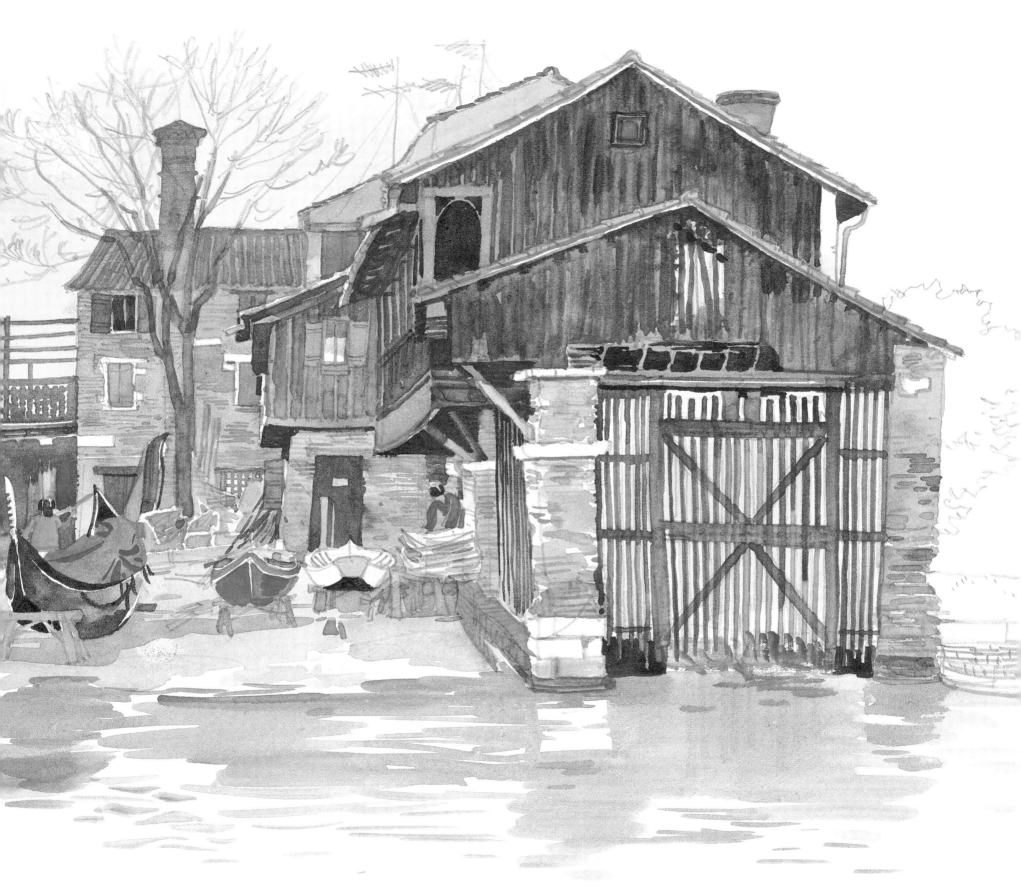

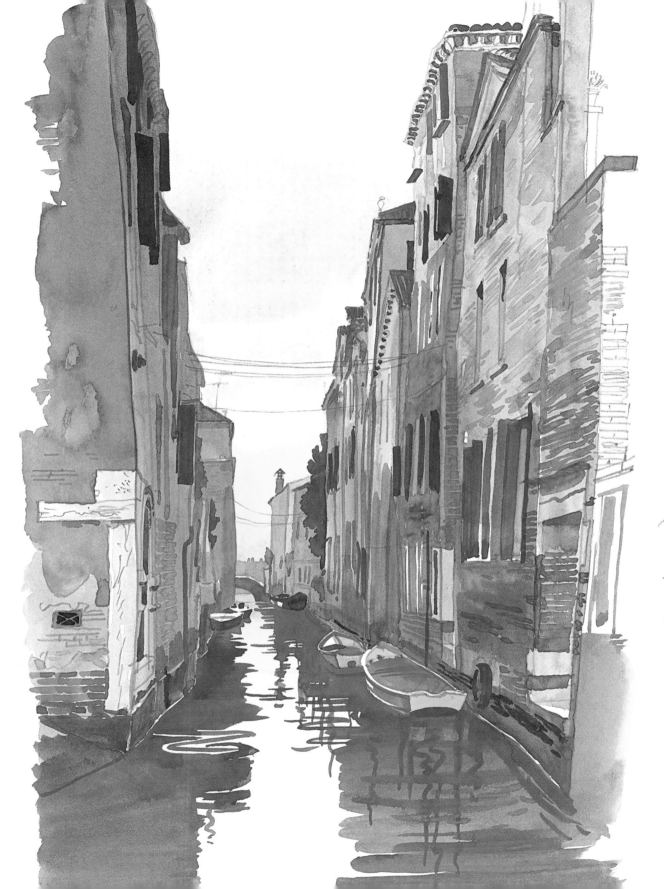

The February sunshine softens
the contours of Rio delle Toreselle,
linking the Grand Canal
to the Giudecca Canal.
It runs behind the Palazzo Venier
dei Leoni, left unfinished due to
pressure from the powerful
Corner family,
whose palace on the other side
of the Grand Canal it would
have overshadowed.
In 1949, Peggy Guggenheim
installed some of her modern
art collection here.

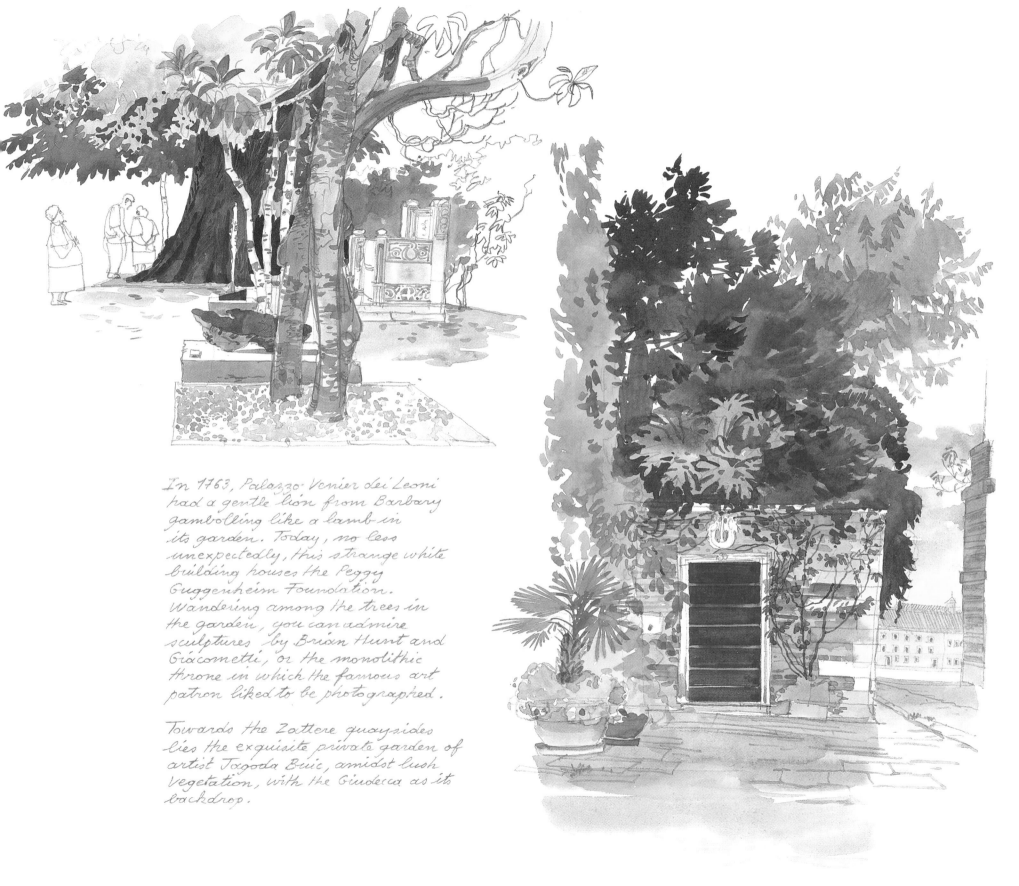

In 1763, Palazzo Venier dei Leoni had a gentle lion from Barbary gambolling like a lamb in its garden. Today, no less unexpectedly, this strange white building houses the Peggy Guggenheim Foundation. Wandering among the trees in the garden, you can admire sculptures by Brian Hunt and Giacometti, or the monolithic throne in which the famous art patron liked to be photographed.

Towards the Zattere quaysides lies the exquisite private garden of artist Jagoda Buic, amidst lush vegetation, with the Giudecca as its backdrop.

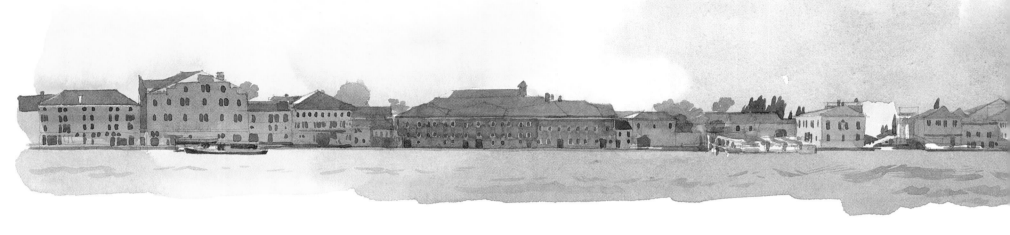

The island of Giudecca.
The Palladian church of the Redentore and
  the Mulino Stucky (a flour mill) dominate
the long waterfront, a line of buildings protecting
  the once-numerous gardens,
including kitchen gardens, from the cruel
  east winds. On the Zattere quaysides opposite,
  Venetians like to come and bask
      in the winter sun.

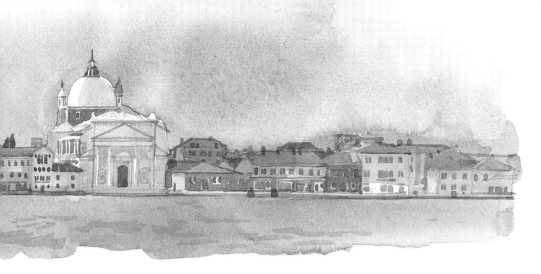

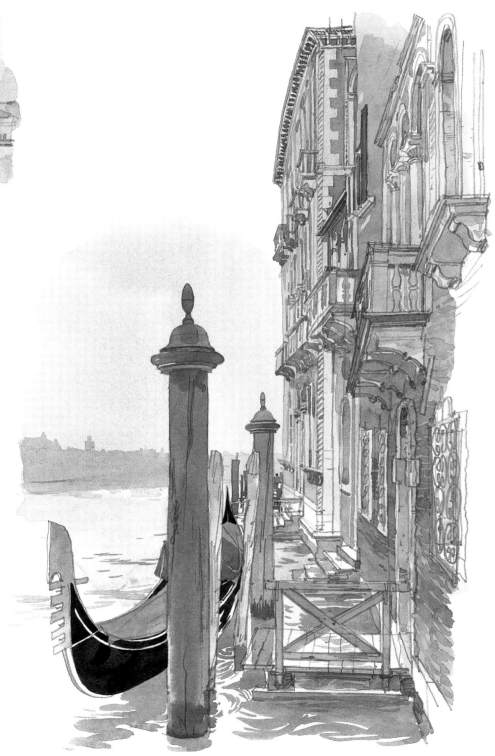

Near Punta della Dogana, overlooking St Mark's docks, a gondola is tied to the "brícole" of a private jetty at the entrance to an imposing palace. Every important Venetian family had its own gondolier "de casada" (personal gondolier), party to all the family secrets. The "brícole" used to be painted in the colours of the family's coat of arms.

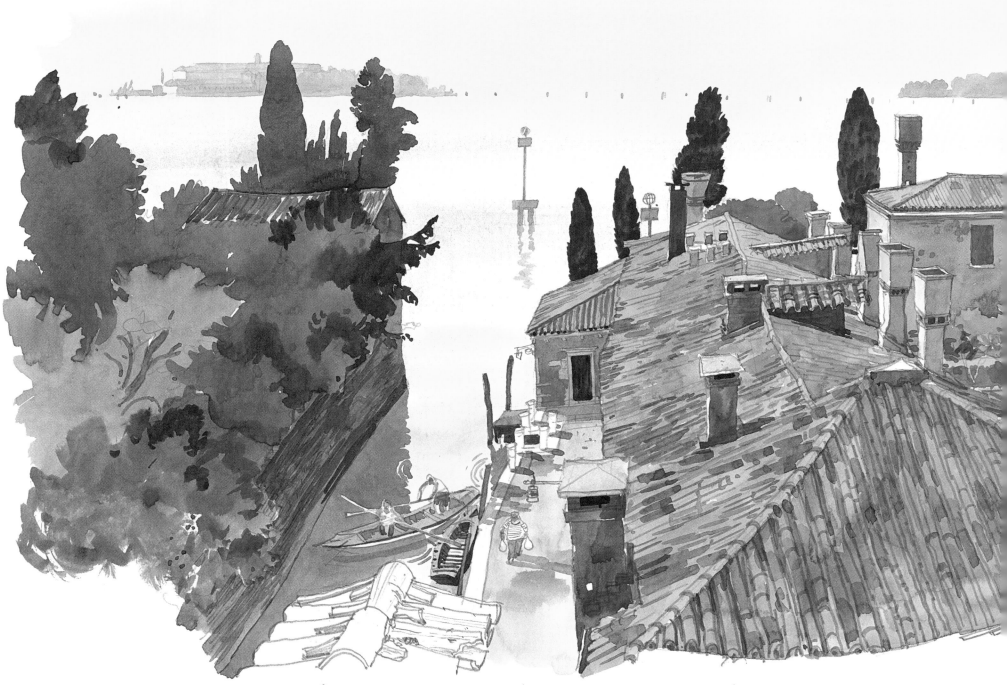

The view from the terraces of the Giudecca, with the cypress trees
of Count Volpi's garden silhouetted against the mirror-like lagoon.
In the distance, the islands of Santa Maria della Grazia and San Clemente.

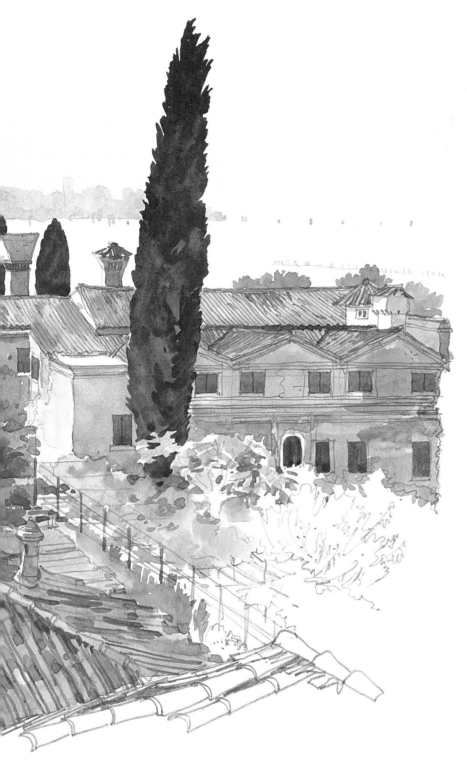

The Islands

In the Middle Ages, towns were protected by high ramparts. Venice had her own natural protection: the lagoon. The maze of canals and small islands, sometimes submerged depending on the tide, held no secrets for the early Venetians. The long spits of land which constitute the Lido and Pellestrina, stretching from Cavallino to Chioggia, protected the city from storms and barbarian invasions. The lagoon's tight huddle of islands, once shelter for boats during violent storms, have gradually become part of the Serenissima.

These islands had a raison d'être: some harboured monasteries and convents, such as Santo Spirito and Sant'Andrea della Certosa; some provided refuge for pilgrims departing for or returning from the Holy Land; others welcomed the sick, like San Lazzaro dei Armeni which became a hospice with the outbreak of leprosy in Venice in the 12th century.

Over the centuries, these island jewels have lost their economic and political importance. Of the lagoon's 34 islands, only half are still inhabited. Some were always deserted, other have been abandoned and deserve to be given new life, as have former military areas and hospitals dating from the Austrian Occupation, which are slowly re-entering the world as religious or conference centres, catering schools or luxury hotels.

Each island is a world unto itself: Poveglia, which has not yet been 'restored', is immediately captivating, with its slender belltower, its strong scent of peach in summer and its protective coat of white acacia flowers. Venetians flock to San Michele to put flowers on the tombs of their dead, turning it into a large and magnificent garden. On Torcello, which once rivalled Venice, and later occupied a special place in the writings of John Ruskin, time seems to have stopped: the few remaining inhabitants, houses half-buried amongst the reeds, abandoned boats and the occasional fisherman all have an air of peaceful melancholy. Burano and its lace, Murano and its glass, the Lido and its beaches all float, as Goethe once wrote, on this 'large liquid mirror which the real Venice, in the shape of a crescent, embraces'.

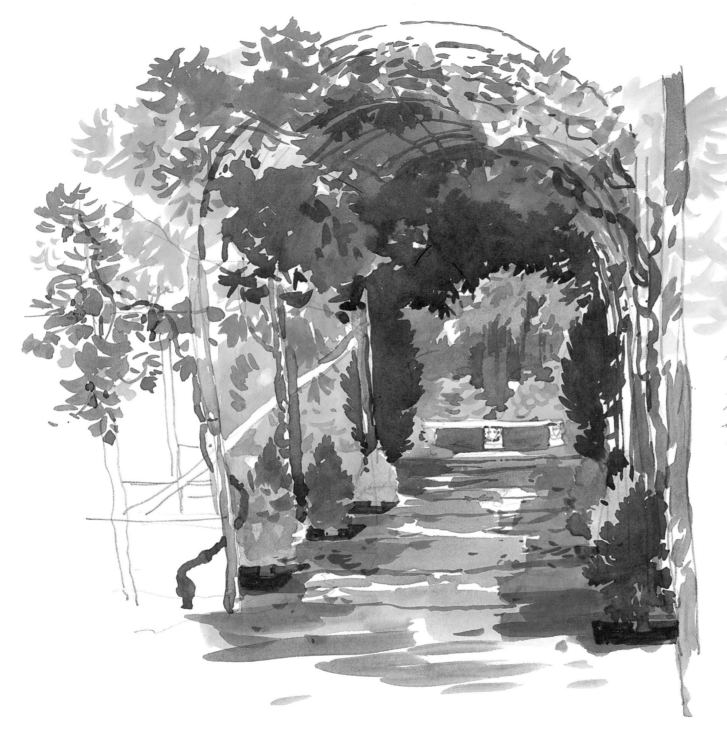

The Casanova garden of
the Hotel Cipriani, at the
eastern end of the Giudeca
is a fine example of a
modern Venetian garden.
The pergolas, laden with
sweet, juicy grapes, are a
perfect setting for the game of
seduction. In the 16th century,
the area overlooking the lagoon
was filled with the exotic plants of
the Dogaressa Loredana Marcello
Mocenigo, while behind it stood the
kitchen garden of the Zitelle
convent, a refuge for fallen women.
Today, Zitelle is just the name of
the "vaporetto" stop.

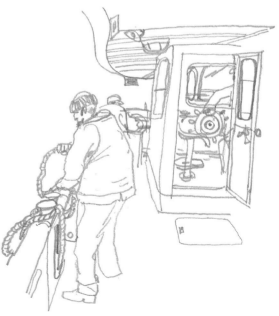

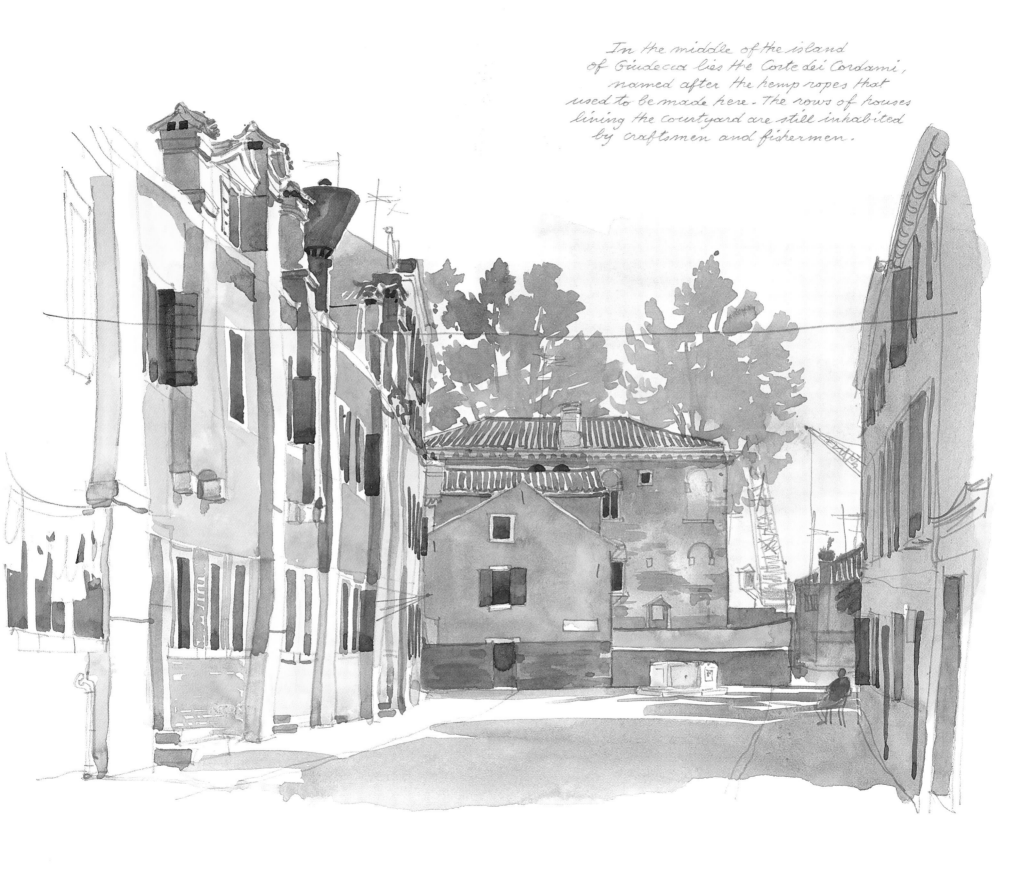

In the middle of the island
of Giudecca lies the Corte dei Cordami,
named after the hemp ropes that
used to be made here. The rows of houses
lining the courtyard are still inhabited
by craftsmen and fishermen.

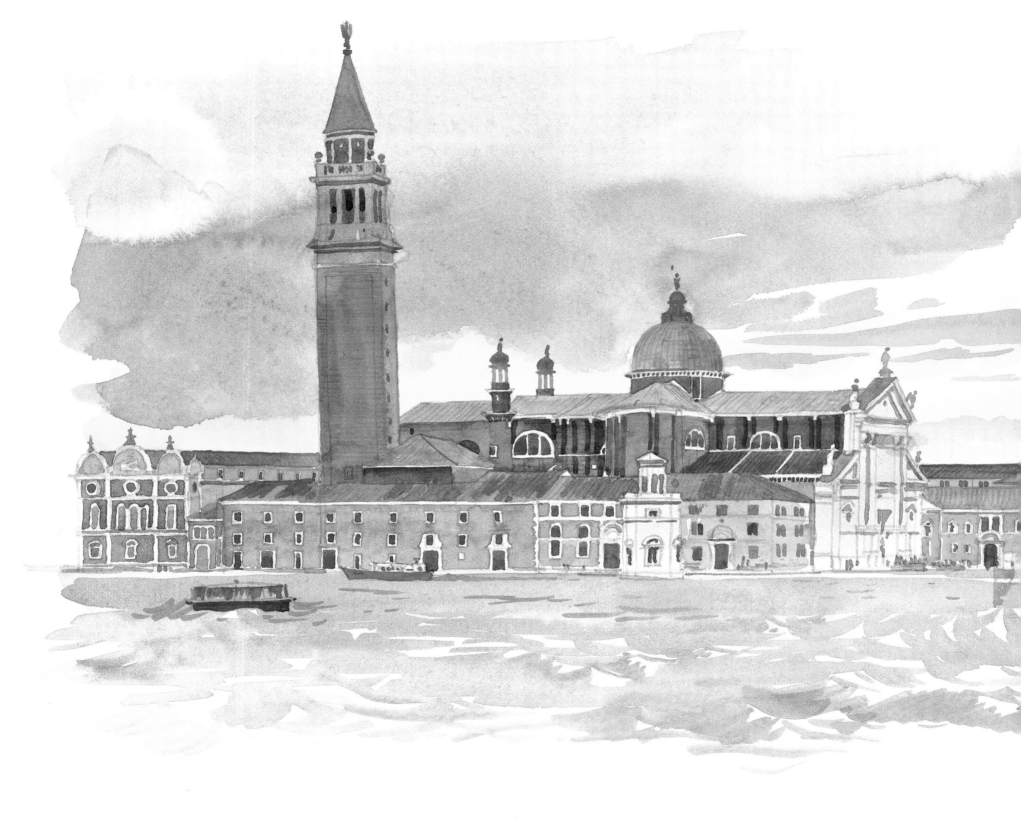

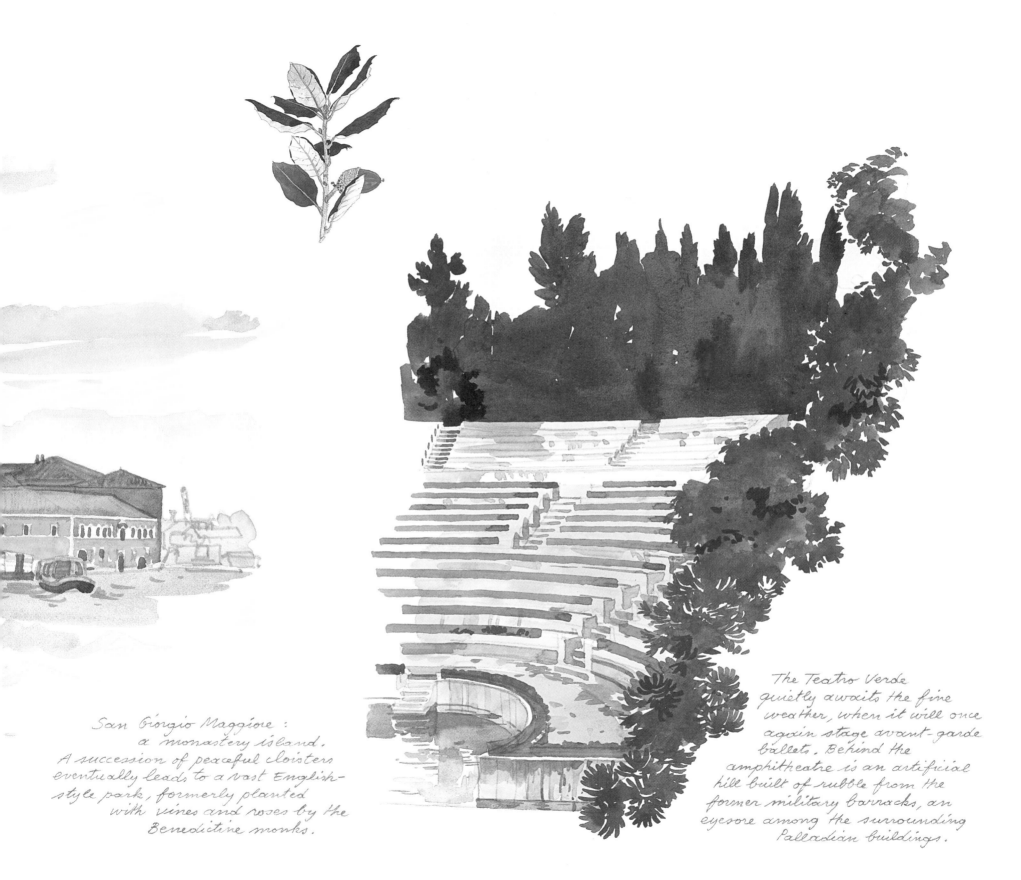

San Giorgio Maggiore:
a monastery island.
A succession of peaceful cloisters
eventually leads to a vast English-
style park, formerly planted
with vines and roses by the
Benedictine monks.

The Teatro Verde
quietly awaits the fine
weather, when it will once
again stage avant-garde
ballets. Behind the
amphitheatre is an artificial
hill built of rubble from the
former military barracks, an
eyesore among the surrounding
Palladian buildings.

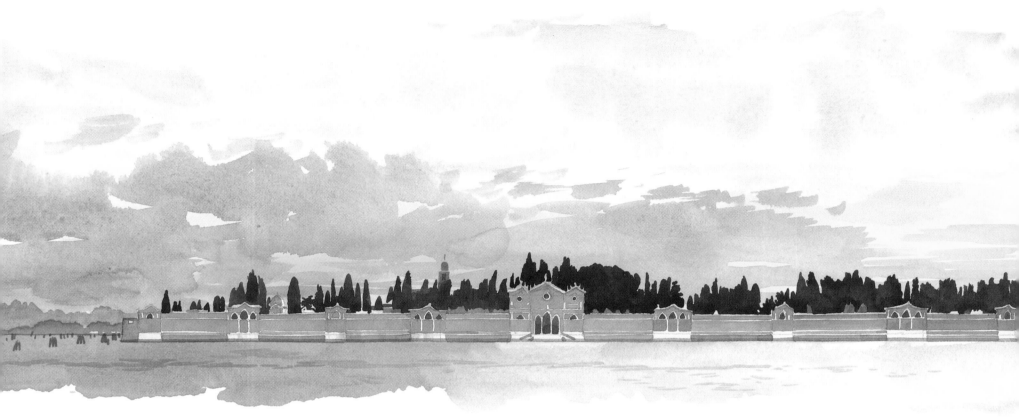

The brick walls of San Michele
cemetery encircle the island, just off the
Fondamente Nuove quayside, with the
foothills of the Alps rising up behind.

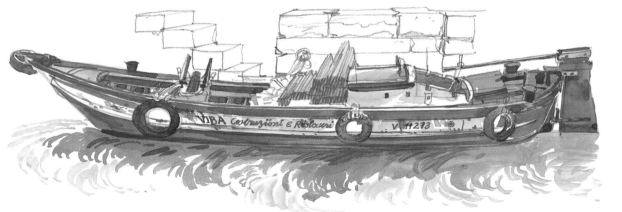

Within the Orthodox section
a priest tends to Diaghilev's tomb,
decorated with ballet shoes.
Stravinsky, at his own
request, is buried along
side the founder of the
Ballets Russes.

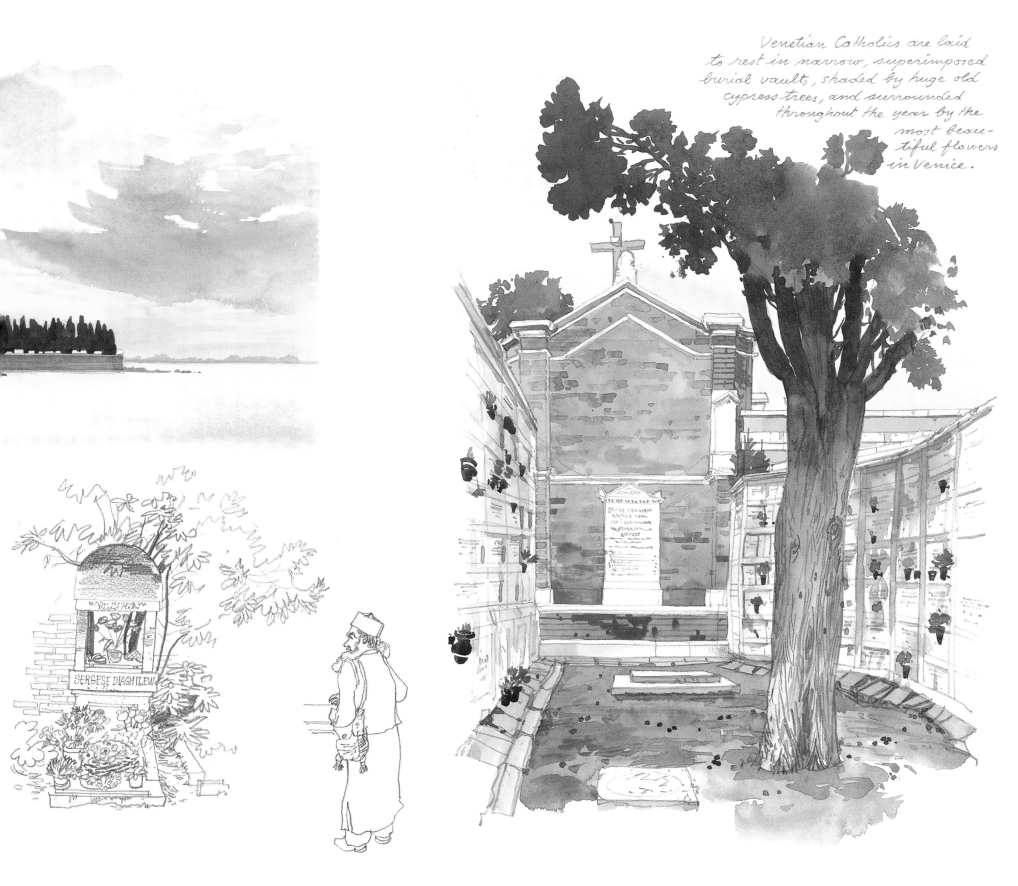

Venetian Catholics are laid
to rest in narrow, superimposed
burial vaults, shaded by huge old
cypress trees, and surrounded
throughout the year by the
most beau-
tiful flowers
in Venice.

SERGESE DIAGHILEW

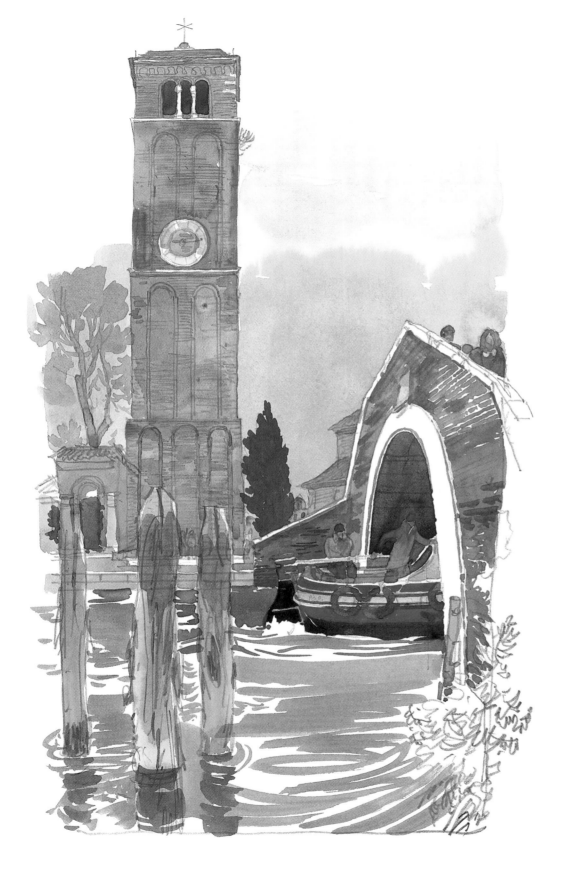

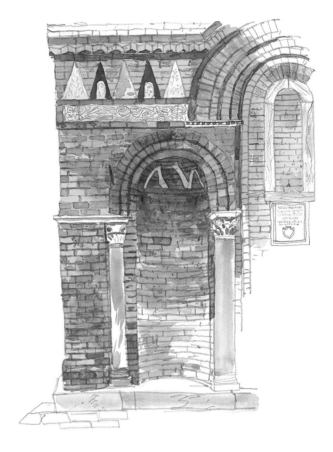

At first sight, the island of Murano looks like a succession of austere, smoke-stained façades.

Sixty glassworks are still in operation, maintaining the island's centuries-old reputation.

The first glassworks were set up here around 1291, transferred from Venice proper, as the fire-risks they engendered were considered too great for the Serenissima.

The Basilica Santa Maria e San Donato, a jewel of Veneto-Byzantine art, shines out in the centre of this "Venice in miniature".

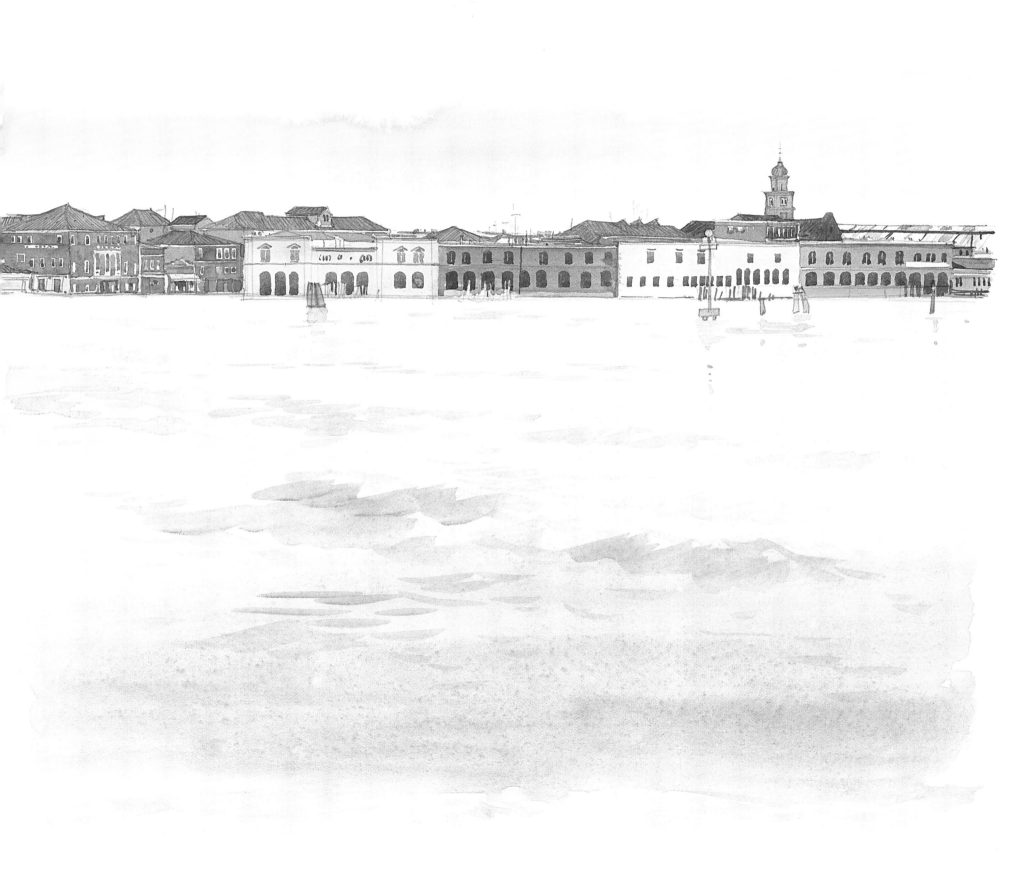

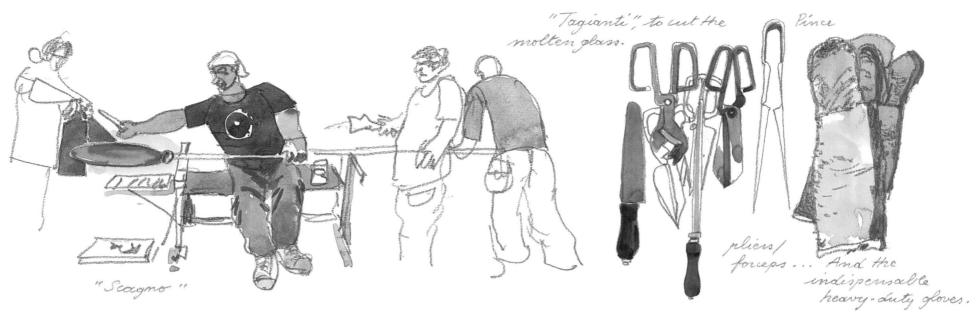

"Tagianti", to cut the molten glass.

Pince

pliers/ forceps ... And the indispensable heavy-duty gloves.

"Scagno"

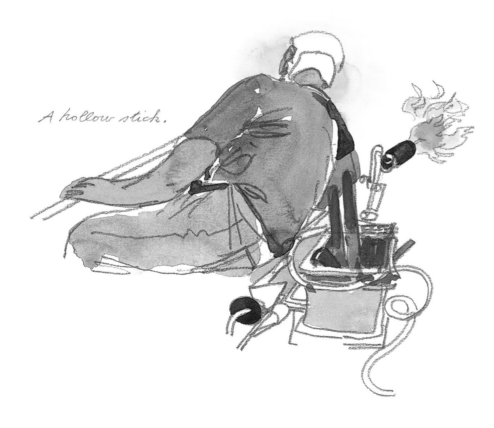

A hollow stick.

In his time-worn hideaway, far-removed from the tourists, master glass-blower Davide Salvadore creates striking contemporary works. Together, he and the glass reinvent tradition, exchanging ancient secrets.
First the maestro rolls a ball of molten glass paste on the "bronzin", an immaculately smooth metal plate. Then, seated at his "scagno" (workbench), surrounded by assistants, he skilfully executes a series of rapid, precise movements and the glass begins to take shape.

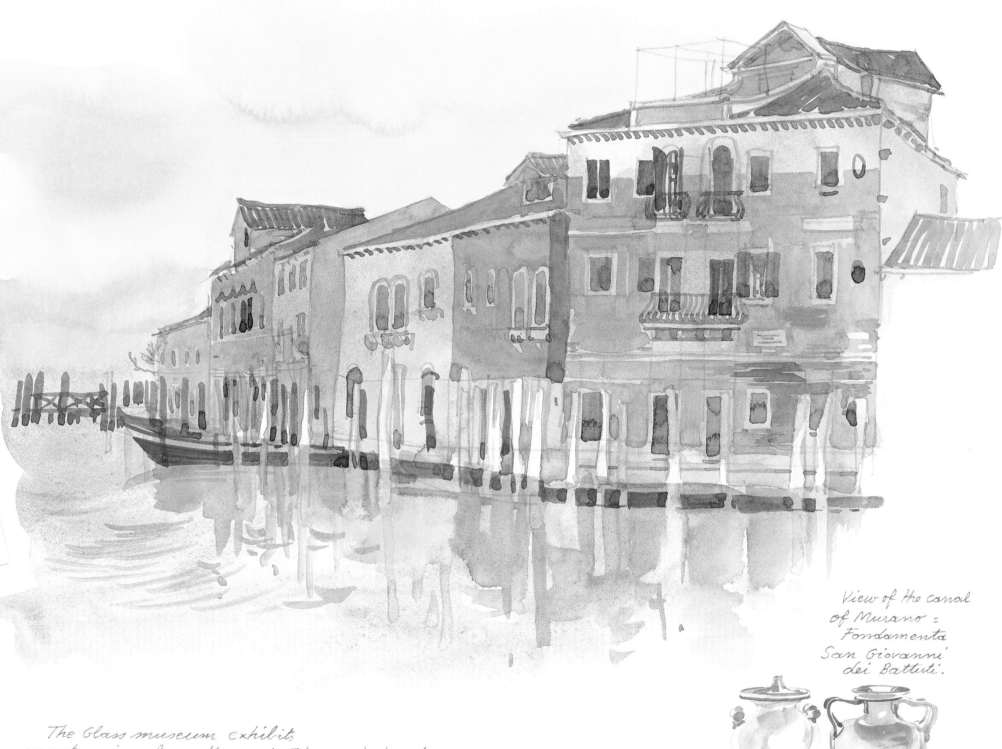

View of the canal
of Murano :
Fondamenta
San Giovanni
dei Battuti.

The Glass museum exhibits
masterpieces from the past. The washed-out
blue of these Roman urns is in perfect harmony
with the colour of the water of the lagoon.
On the opposite side of the canal is Palazzo Trevisan, a masterpiece
of Renaissance art, adorned with frescoes by Veronese.

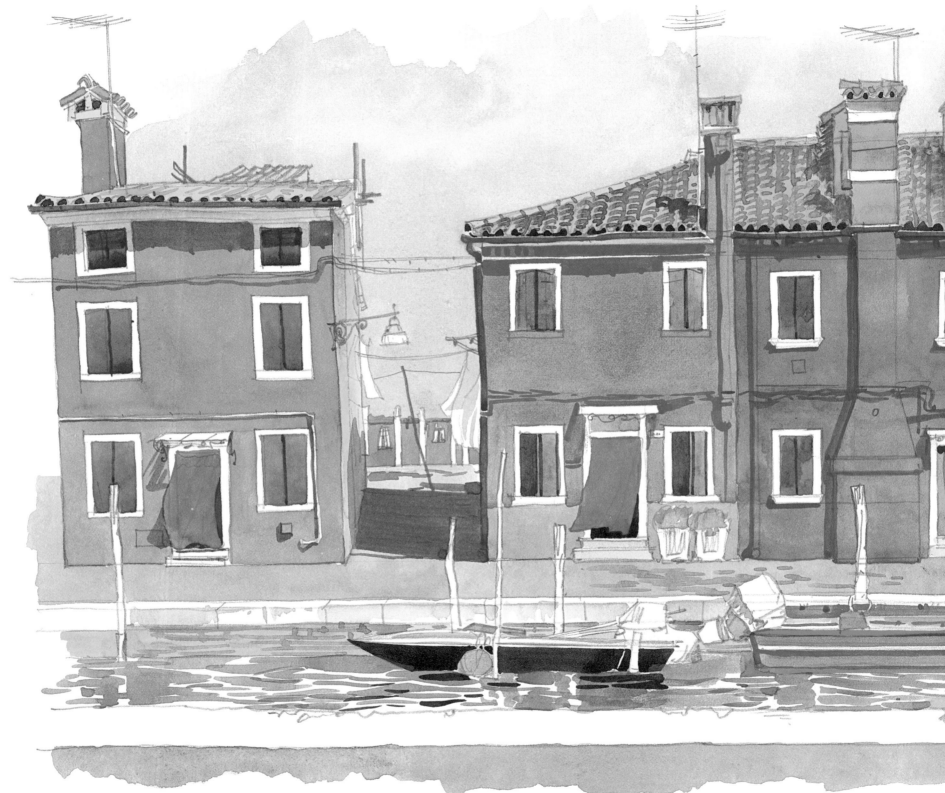

Burano. Lining the quayside, these rainbow-coloured fishermen's houses make a gay, almost unreal townscape, inspiration for generations of artists.

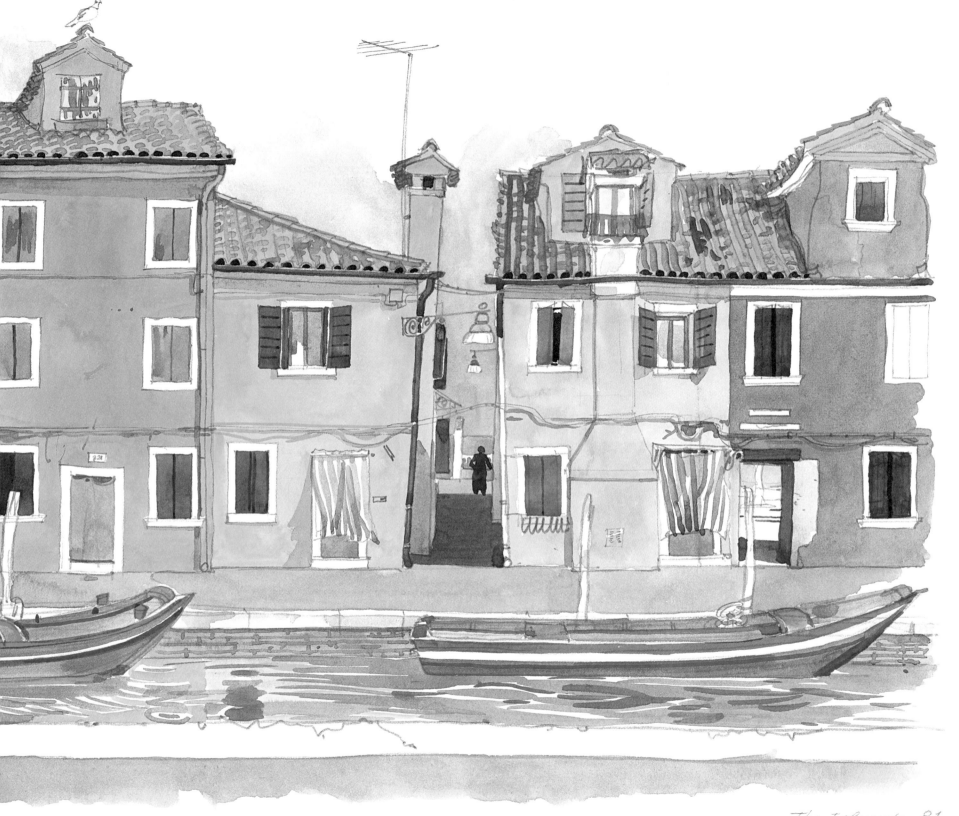

The Islands 81

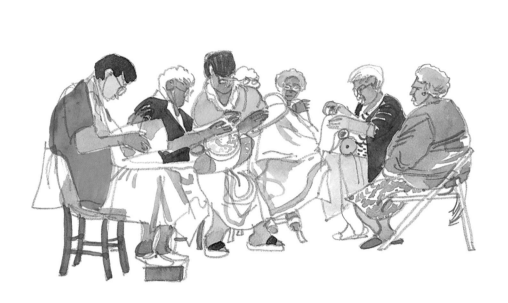

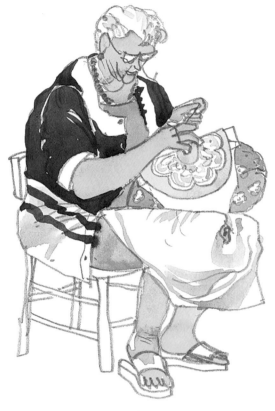

Every year, during Holy Week,
the women repaint their houses in the
same bright colours used for the fishing boats.
          Their kitchens are transplanted
on to the quayside : the perfect
opportunity to savour the best grilled
                sardines in the world !
          At the end of the day, these same
women don their lacemaking caps.
          Sitting in their doorways, they deftly
ply their needles, creating the
intricately delicate lace for which the
          island is famous.

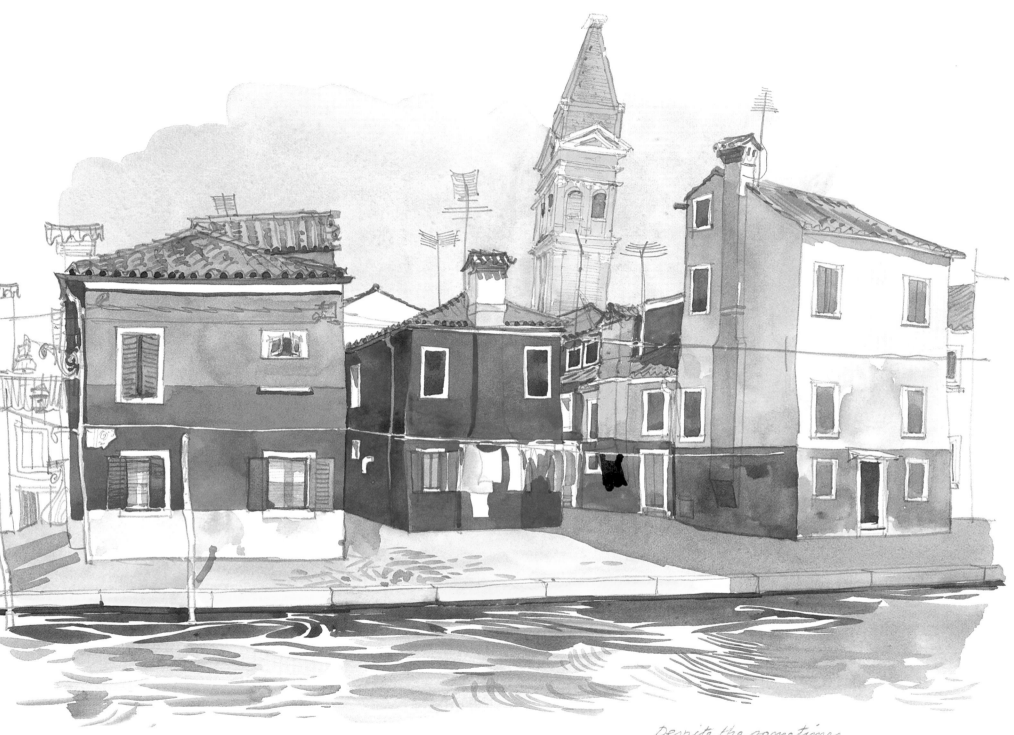

Despite the sometimes
overwhelming presence of tourists,
life on Burano is quite calm, with
its small squares strung across
with peacefully drying washing.
Only the bell-tower leans
rather ominously.

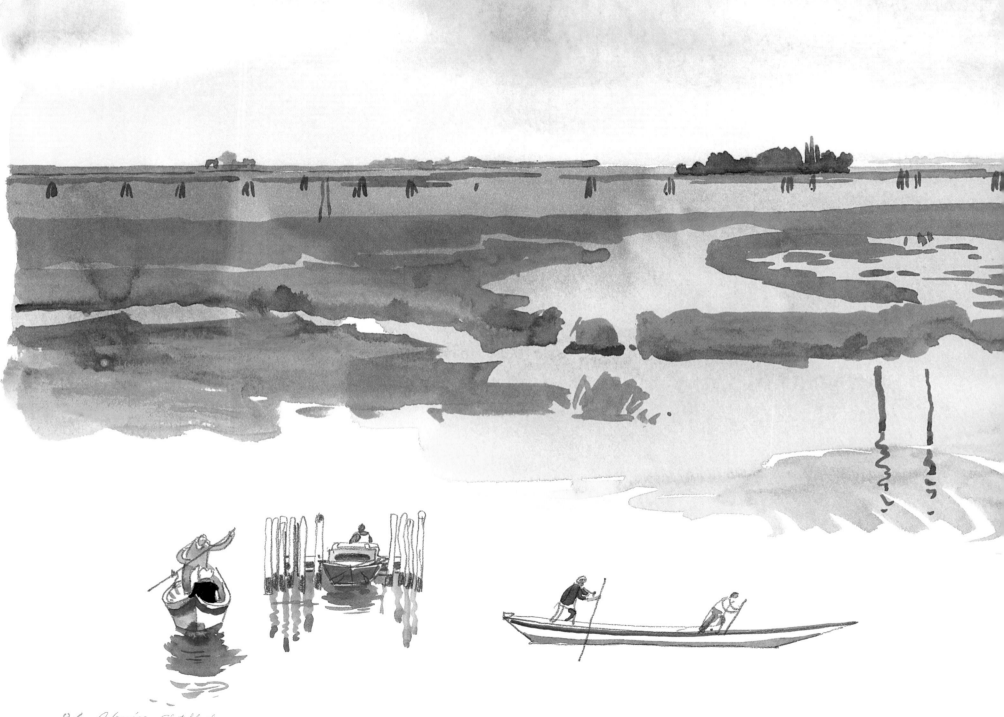

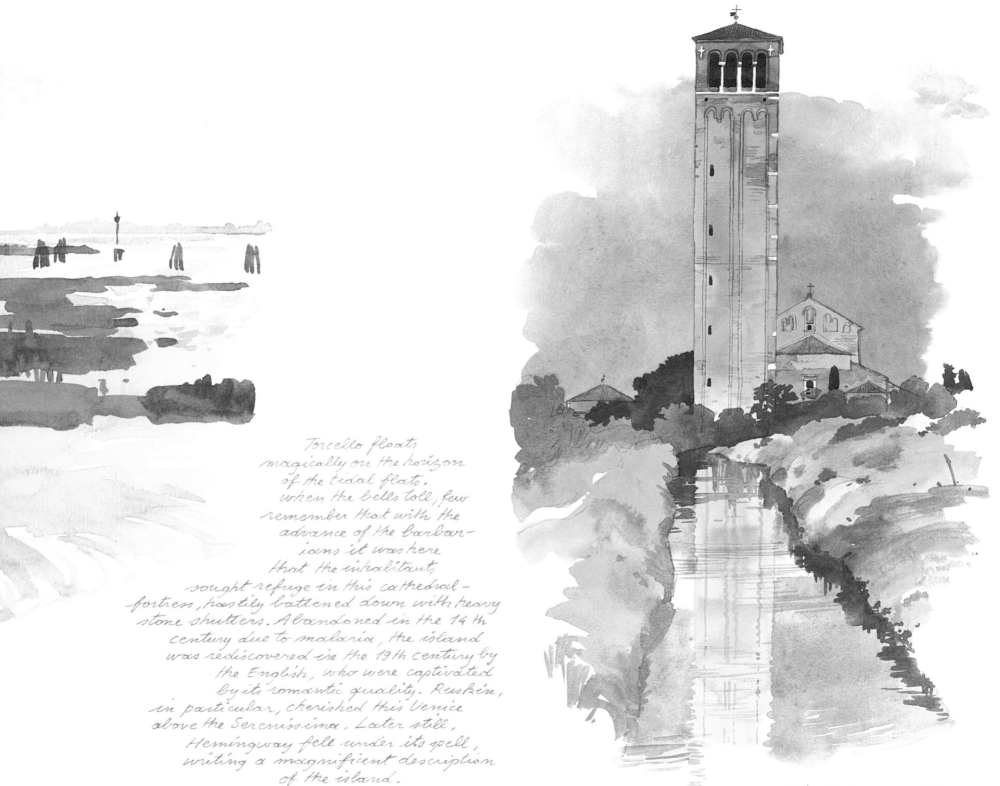

Torcello floats
magically on the horizon
of the tidal flats.
When the bells toll, few
remember that with the
advance of the barbar-
ians it was here
that the inhabitants,
sought refuge in this cathedral-
fortress, hastily battened down with heavy
stone shutters. Abandoned in the 14th
century due to malaria, the island
was rediscovered in the 19th century by
the English, who were captivated
by its romantic quality. Ruskin,
in particular, cherished this Venice
above the Serenissima. Later still,
Hemingway fell under its spell,
writing a magnificent description
of the island.

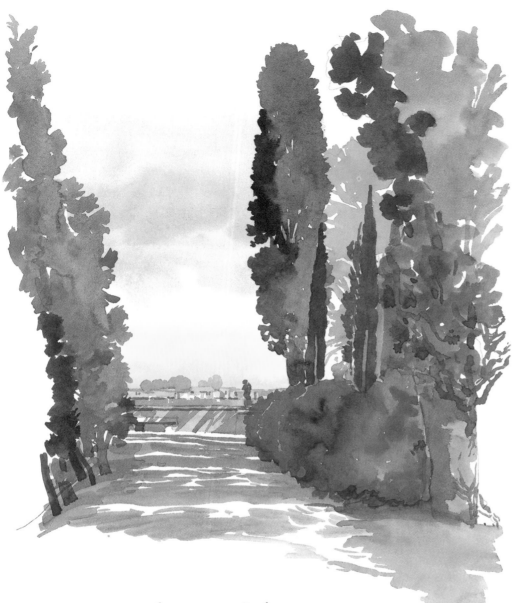

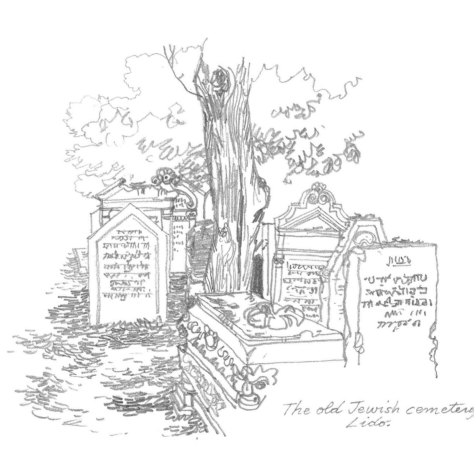

On the island of
Sant' Erasmo,
in front of San Francesco
del Deserto, tender,
purple-hued early
artichokes, known as
"castraure"
have been cultivated
since Roman times.

A few oar-strokes south
of Burano is the low-lying, sleepy
monastery island of San Francesco
del Deserto. Surrounded by the
lagoon's birdlife, the monks
still live according to the rules of
their founder, dressed in habits tied
at the waist with a white cord.

The old Jewish cemetery,
Lido.

The Lido

The long, sandy spit shielding the lagoon from
the full force of the Adriatic, still has its own special
hidden places. The old Jewish cemetery, near the Benedictine
monastery of San Nicolo del Lido, is one of the most moving.

Alfred de Musset and George Sand used to walk
here in 1834, amongst the tombs of Jewish families who had
fled Spain under Philip II. The Doge used to cross the lagoon
in his own vessel, the "Bucintoro",
to attend a grand
mass at San Nicolo
in celebration of
Venice's betrothal
to the sea.

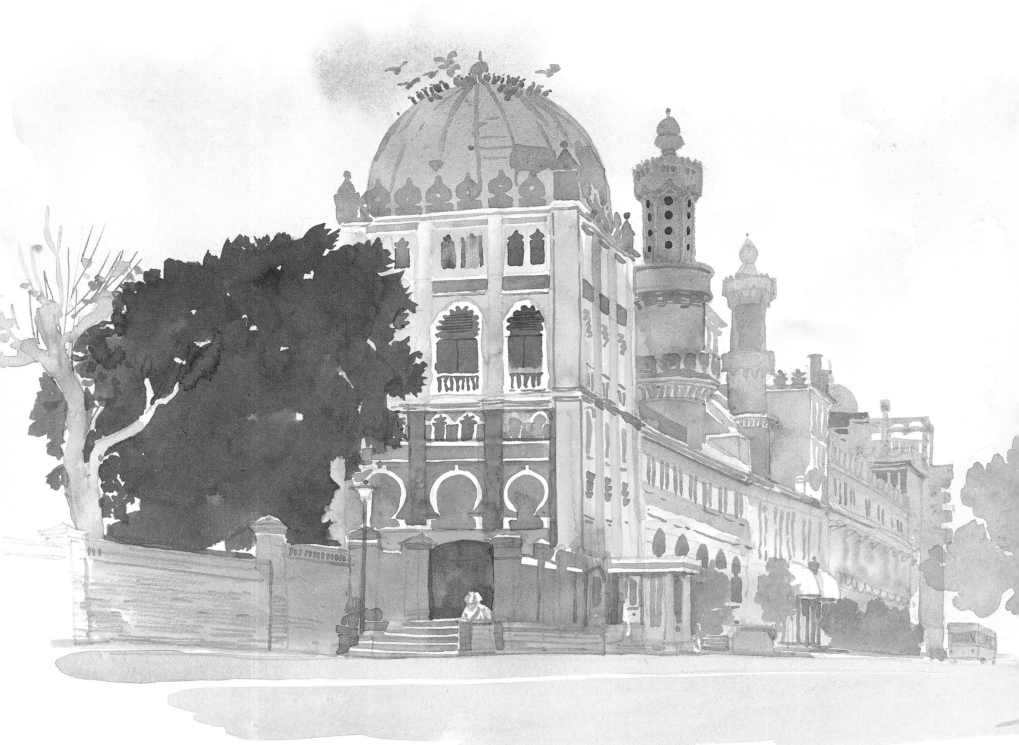

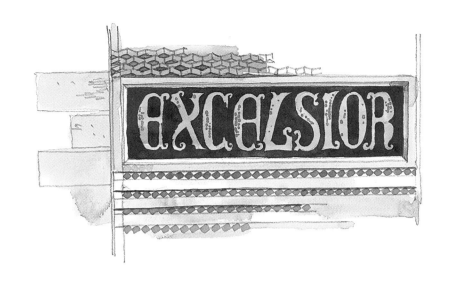

Hotel Excelsior, the oldest
and the most prestigious
of the Lido hotels, was built
between 1898 and 1908,
following designs by
Giovanni Sardi. Architectur-
ally it typifies the Venetian's
infatuation with the Orient.
Between the World Wars, both
the international jet set and
film-lovers flocked here,
caught up in an endless
round of hedonistic festivity.

On the beach, in front of the hotel,
children amass their seaside treasure:
pinkish, mother-of-pearl bivalves,
geometric-shaped "garusoli", blue-tinted
"peoci" and other bizarre creatures washed up
by the sea.

The Islands   89

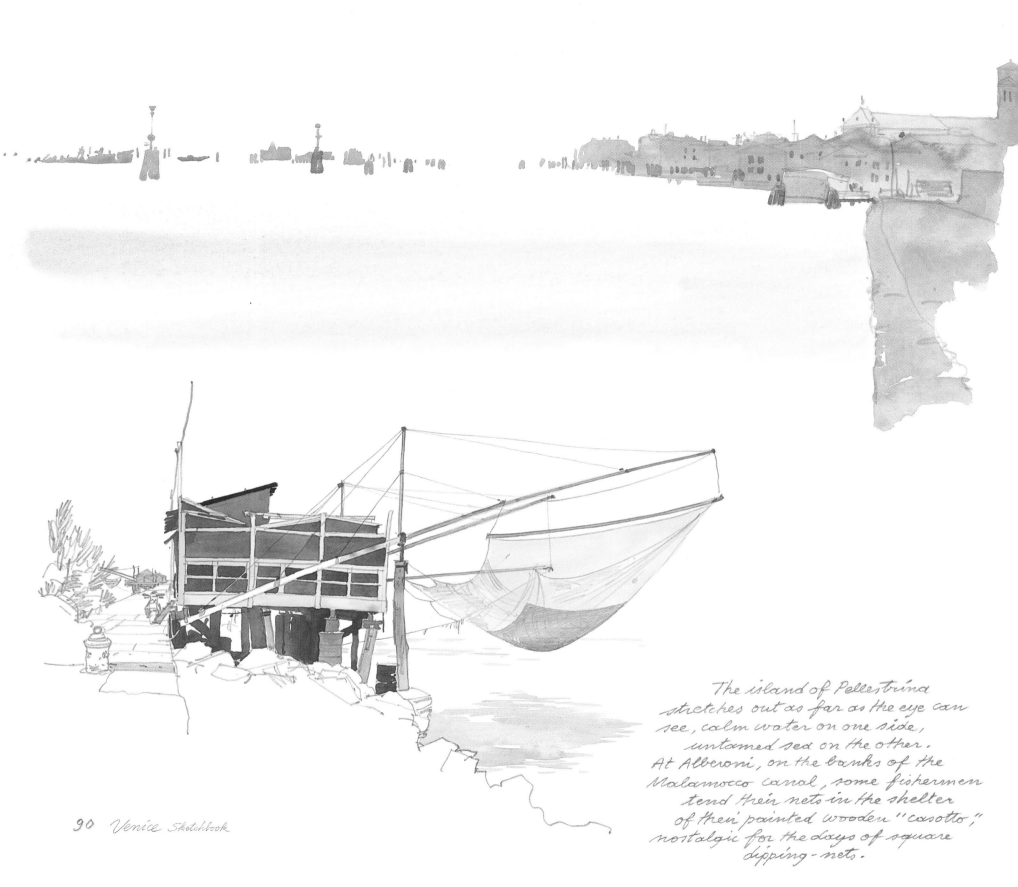

The island of Pellestrina
stretches out as far as the eye can
see, calm water on one side,
untamed sea on the other.
At Alberoni, on the banks of the
Malamocco canal, some fishermen
tend their nets in the shelter
of their painted wooden "casotto,"
nostalgic for the days of square
dipping-nets.

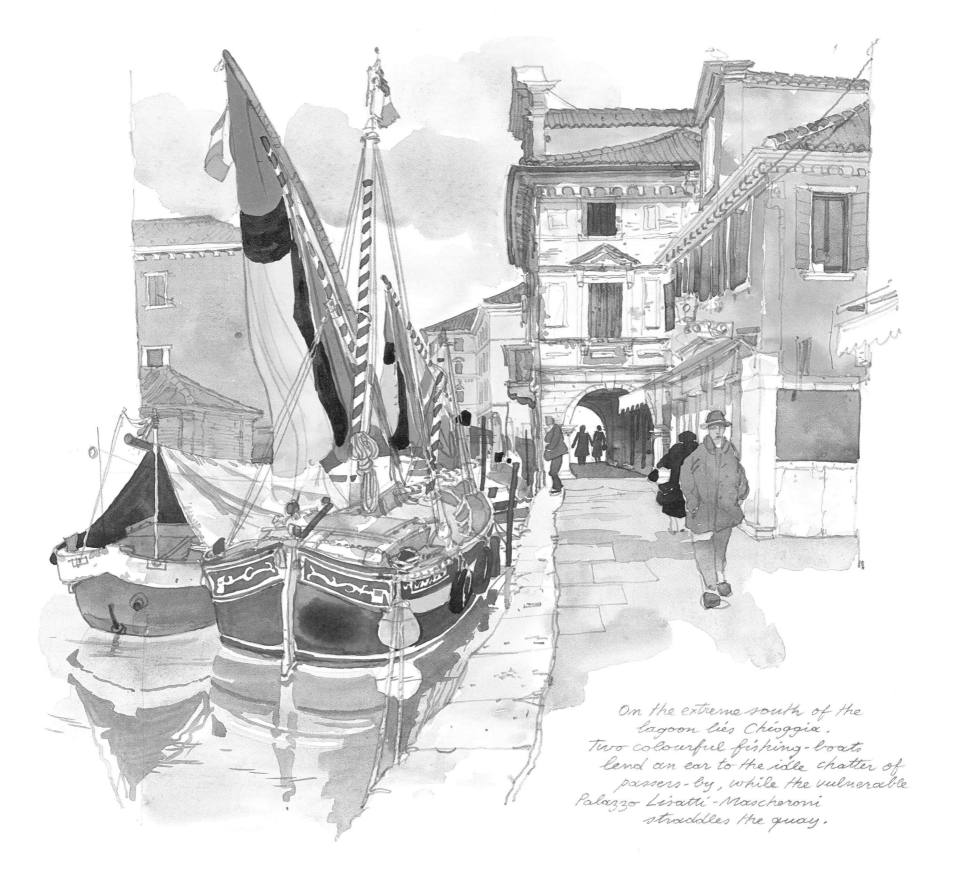

On the extreme south of the
lagoon lies Chioggia.
Two colourful fishing-boats
lend an ear to the idle chatter of
passers-by, while the vulnerable
Palazzo Lisatti-Mascheroni
straddles the quay.

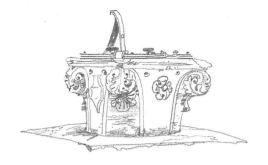

Gazetteer

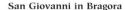

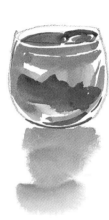

San Giovanni in Bragora
The church of San Giovanni in Bragora – the name derives from the Greek *agora* meaning market-place – was founded in the early 8th century by Saint Magno, Bishop of Oderzo. The façade was reconstructed at the end of the 15th century and gracefully echoes the curvilinear form of the fine Gothic interior. The elegant arcaded bell-tower was built in 1728, to replace the previous one, destroyed by an earthquake.

The Arsenal gateway
The gateway, erected in 1460 during the reign of Doge Pasquale Malipiero, is based on the Porta Aurea, the Roman Triumphal Arch of Sergius in Pula, Istria, and is one of the earliest Renaissance monuments in Venice. Under the threat of Turkish expansion after the fall of Constantinople in 1453, it was decided to expand the Arsenal shipyards. As early as 1473, the additional eight hectares which made up the Arsenale Nuovissimo provided wet-docks for up to eighty galleys.

San Pietro di Castello
The church we see today dates back to 1596 and was built by Francesco Smeraldi, based on a model by Andrea Palladio. San Pietro di Castello was Venice's cathedral until 1807, when it was supplanted by St Mark's.

San Francesco della Vigna
Not far from Campo Ugo Foscolo, lies the Church of San Francesco della Vigna, named after the vine given to the Franciscans by Marco Ziani, son of Doge Pietro Ziani, in 1253. The present church, built in 1534, is the work of Jacopo Sansovino. The Palladio façade was added later. According to legend, an ancient chapel was built in the vineyard, on the exact spot where an angel had addressed St Mark, recently arrived from Aquileia en route for Rome: 'Pax tibi, Marce, evangelista meus' (Peace be with you, oh Mark, my evangelist). These words subsequently became the Serenissima's motto.

Santa Maria Formosa
Probably dating back to the 7th century, this is one of the eight oldest churches in Venice. The present church is the work of Mauro Codussi and was built in 1492 on top of the earlier foundations. Santa Maria Formosa was home to several *scuole* (philanthropic-cum-trade guild confraternities), including the Scuola dei Bombardieri (cannon-makers), whose chapel, dedicated to St Barbara, houses a painting by Palma Vecchio, and the Scuola dei Casseleri, makers of wedding chests for the dowries of brides-to-be.

Santi Giovanni e Paolo
The construction of the Church of Santi Giovanni e Paolo began in the middle of the 13th century, on land given to the Dominicans by Doge Jacopo Tiepolo. It continued for over two centuries and the façade remains incomplete. Nevertheless, it is one of the finest examples of Flamboyant Gothic in Venice and demonstrates a perfect balance between the building's length (101 m) and its exceptional height (55 m to the top of the dome). Built in the form of a Latin cross, the interior is bathed in light thanks to the five magnificent pierced-stone apses. Fine examples of Venetian sculpture are seen in the funerary monuments adorning the walls of this important basilica.

St Mark's Basilica
The first church was built between 829 and 832 by the family of Doge Partecipazio as a sanctuary for St Mark's remains and as a chapel for the Doge's Palace. It was destroyed by fire in 976 and subsequently rebuilt. Between 1063 and 1073, reflecting Venice's ever-growing power, Doge Contarini had it enlarged, using the 4th-century Church of the Apostle-Saints in Byzantium as a source of inspiration. The façades and domes were added between the 12th and 14th centuries. Altogether they form a magnificent example of the successful marriage of Byzantine, Romanesque and Gothic styles. This marble building at the foot of the Campanile was built between 1537 and 1549 by Sansovino as the guards' headquarters. After the collapse of the Campanile in 1902, it was rebuilt exactly as before. Three of the composite arcades are decorated with statues and bas-reliefs. The Loggetta is situated on an axis with the Porta della Carta and the Scala dei Giganti.

Porta della Carta
The Porta della Carta is the main entrance to the Doge's Palace, constructed between 1438 and 1441 by Giovanni and Bartolomeo Bon, father and son. It is a masterpiece of polychrome marble 'lacework', neatly linking the Palace and the Basilica.

St Mark's Square Café
At one time there were 26 cafés on St Mark's Square, lively meeting places and cultural venues. On 29 December 1720, under the arcades of the Procuratie Nuove, Floriano Francesconi opened Venezia Trionfante – subsequently known as Caffè Florian – which soon became a famous Venetian institution. In 1858, Lodovico Cadorin lavished on it the refined decor still visible today: each salon is decorated with paintings and mirrors representing a different theme: the Room of the Illustrious Men, the Room of Seasons, the Oriental Room, the Chinese Room…

The Bridge of Sighs
The Bridge of Sighs was built by decree of the Senate in 1600, under the authority of Doge Marino Grimani, whose coat of arms adorns the construction. This suspended arch of Istrian stone is the work of Antonio Contino. It derives its name from the sighs emanating from the prisoners contemplating the lagoon for the last time as they walked across it to be tried by the State Inquisitors.

Prigioni Nuove (New Prisons)
The palace overlooks the canal, opposite the Doge's Palace. Designed by Antonio da Ponte at the end of the 16th century, this imposing building, made of Istrian stone, has a vast internal courtyard. It was formerly the headquarters of the Signori di Notte al Criminale, a sort of nightwatch brigade. Today it houses the Circolo Artistico.

Sant'Apollonia's Cloister
Belonging to the Primiceri, the priests of St Mark's, this 12th–13th-century cloister is the only Romanesque example of its kind in Venice. The doorway is encircled by small arches supported by delicate twin columns, beyond which lies the Museo Diocesano.

Palazzo Contarini del Bovolo
Completed in 1499, this palace is attributed to Giovanni Candi. The main façade is particularly unusual for Venice: a spiral staircase housed within an open round tower leads to a loggia, from where there is a spectacular view of the city. The light and airy structure of this stairwell is the perfect fusion of Gothic and Renaissance architecture. Its form seems to have so impressed the locals that the name 'Bovolo' ('spiral' in Venetian) was not only given to the staircase, but also to the family to whom the palace belonged!

Palazzo Pesaro degli Orfei
Palazzo Pesaro degli Orfei is one of the largest palaces in Venice. It is also one of the most important examples of Venetian Late Gothic, as seen both in its overall unity of structure and in the stylistic coherence of its façades. Now known as Palazzo Fortuny, it houses the foundation of the famous painter and stylist, Mariano Fortuny y Madrazo (1871-1949), displaying collections of his paintings, fabrics and theatre models.

Palazzo Barbaro
The palace dates from the 15th century and opens onto Campo Santo Stefano on one side and the Grand Canal on another; its ogival architecture, typical of the period, is based on that of the Doge's Palace.

Palazzo Falier
This picturesque Gothic building dates from the 15th century. William Dean Howells lived on one floor of the palace from 1862 to 1864. American Consul to Venice, he was one of the first foreign writer to be interested in the daily life of Venetians.

Santa Maria del Giglio
This church was constructed between 1678 and 1683, by Giuseppe Sardi, in honour of the Barbaro family, and has a richly decorative Baroque façade. The statues in the niches represent the ship-captain Antonio Barbaro and his four brothers; the strange bas-reliefs illustrate military and civic virtues.

The Fenice Theatre
The theatre was erected between 1790 and 1792 by Gianantonio Selva, on the site of the San Benedetto theatre which burnt down in 1774. The building is surprisingly complex for such a young architect: the narrowness of the façade overlooking Campo San Fantin gives no hint of the immensity of the horse-shoe-shaped auditorium, renowned for its perfect accoustics, which can seat up to 1,500 spectators. When the theatre burnt down the first time in 1836, the Meduna brothers managed to rebuild an exact replica within eight months. After the fire of 29 January 1996, architect Aldo Rossi, put in charge of its reconstruction, made audiences wait nearly eight years, until 14 December 2003, before attending the renaissance of this mythical theatre.

Harry's Bar

In 1929, Giuseppe Cipriani lent 1,000 lira to an American student, Harry Pickering, to enable him to buy his passage back home. On 13 May 1931, with the repaid debt, Cipriani opened a bar in a former rope warehouse at the end of the Calle Vallaresso, right in front of the vaporetto jetty, and named it after his friend. It was an immediate success. The whole world has sat, and continues to sit, in Harry's Bar: Hemingway, Truman Capote, Orson Welles, Maria Callas...

Ponte dei Tre Archi

Built by Andrea Tirali in 1688, this is the sole remaining triple-arch bridge in Venice. It spans the Cannaregio Canal, which used to have many an ambassadorial cortège passing down it en route to the Doge's Palace. On its banks, Palazzo Labia and Palazzo Savorgnan still stand proudly, their respective coats of arms adorning the quayside.

Ca'd'Oro

The Ca'd'Oro was built between 1421 and 1443 by Lombard and Venetian workmen under the direction of Matteo Raverti and Giovanni and Bartolomeo Bon. The façade overlooking the Grand Canal, decorated with polychrome marble highlit with gold (hence its name of Golden House), now almost completely faded, is undoubtedly one of the finest examples of Venetian Flamboyant Gothic.

Palazzo Sagredo

Situated near the Church of Santa Sofia, the palace dates from the 14th century. Its façade still bears traces of an earlier Byzantine gallery of trilobe ogival arches, predecessors of the multiple openings of Late Gothic architecture.

Santa Maria dei Miracoli

One of the earliest examples of the Renaissance to be seen in Venice, this church was constructed between 1481 and 1489 by Pietro Lombardo to house a reputedly miraculous Virgin by Nicolo di Pietro. Its three-part façade is completely decorated with polychrome marble.

Palazzo Labia

One of the most sumptuous 17th-century buildings in Venice, Palazzo Labia is famous for its Tiepolo frescoes and richly-decorated interiors. Two of its façades – one by Alessandro Tremignon overlooking the square and the other by Andrea Cominelli overlooking the canal – were inspired by the work of Baldassare Longhena.

Church of the Madonna dell'Orto

Facing Palazzo del Cammello, the Church of the Madonna dell'Orto was built during the 14th and 15th centuries. Its red-brick façade is a fine example of Venetian Gothic. The niches in the frieze along the rooftops of the side aisles contain statues of the twelve apostles by the workshop of Dalle Masegne. Tintoretto, who lived nearby, painted a number of pictures for the church, and his body lies at rest in one of the absidal chapels.

The Ghetto

'The Jews will live altogether in the houses within the Ghetto. And, so that they may not move about at night, we decree that two gates will be erected, one on the side of the Ghetto Vecchio by the little bridge, and the other on the other side of this bridge, which will be opened at dawn and closed at midnight, under the surveillance of four guardians engaged for this very task, appointed by the Jews themselves for a fee deemed appropriate by our College.' Thus read the first lines of the decree of 29 March 1516 which founded the Ghetto. The area remained cut off from the rest of the city in this way for three centuries.

San Giacomo dell'Orio

Founded in 976, the Church of San Giacomo dell'Orio was rebuilt in the 13th century. Its initial groundplan was transformed by the addition of a transept. The 16th-century wooden coffered ceiling resembles an upturned ship's hull. The Veneto-Byzantine bell-tower dates from the 12th century.

Fondaco dei Turchi

Constructed in the first half of the 13th century, the building was acquired by the Republic in 1381 on behalf of the Marchese di Ferrara, Nicolo V. Its interior was so luxurious that Venetian noblemen regularly borrowed the place to house illustrious guests. From 1628 to 1838, the building was the residence and warehouse of Turkish merchants. Subsequently abandoned, it was bought by the city in 1860, and became home to the Museum of Natural History in 1924. It is the only example of a Veneto-Byzantine house, with corner towers, large doorways on the ground floor, loggias on the upper floor and crenellated end ornaments. The contrasting light and the richness of the marble facing give the building a most refined and elegant air.

Scuola Grande di San Rocco

The Scuola Grande di San Rocco was built between 1515 and 1560 by three different architects: Bartolomeo Bon, Sante Lombardo and Scarpagnino. The overall plan, the rectangular room on the top floor and the ground floor with its double windows echoing those by Codussi, were drawn up by Bartolomeo Bon who was subsequently replaced by Sante Lombardo. Scarpagnino finished off the façade with its double row of Corinthian columns, loosely based on Sansovino's project for the Scuola della Misericordia, and built the imposing staircase linking the two rooms containing Tintoretto's paintings, executed by the artist between 1564 and 1588.

Santa Maria Gloriosa dei Frari

This Franciscan church was founded in the 14th century and rebuilt in the following century. It is a large red-brick building, with massive pillars dividing its façade into three sections. It resembles the Church of Santi Giovanni e Paolo both in size and style, and like its contemporary, houses many important funerary monuments. Some of the city's precious archives are conserved in the former convent, a vast building with the first lodge to be built in the 17th century.

San Cassiano

Originally built in the 10th century, the Church of San Cassiano has undergone numerous transformations, the most recent dating from the early 18th century. The exterior has remained untouched, except for the doorway, which was destroyed in the middle of the 19th century. The church possesses three paintings by Tintoretto.

The Rialto Bridge

This famous bridge was constructed between 1588 and 1592, to replace a wooden bridge which opened in the middle to let boats pass up the Grand Canal. Many of the greatest architects of the time put forward their designs: Palladio, Scamozzi and even, according to Vasari, Michelangelo; but, after many years of deliberation, the Signoria chose Antonio da Ponte. Until the 19th century the resulting construction remained the sole bridge on the Grand Canal.

La Pescheria

This fishmarket was build in 1907 by architects Cesare Laurenti and Domenico Rupolo, after much polemic. It is resolutely Neo-Gothic in style.

Santa Maria della Salute

The Church of Santa Maria della Salute was built between 1631 and 1681 in thanks for the end of the terrible plague of 1630. Eleven proposals were considered for this project; the Senate finally opted for the one by the young Baldassare Longhena. His design was inspired by one of Francesco Colonna's drawings in his *Hypnerotomachia Polyphili* (Polyphilus' Dream), published by Aldo Manuzio in Venice in 1499. Constructed at the entrance to the Grand Canal, the church dominates the Venetian landscape. Monumental steps lead up to the main entrance. Reigning supreme within the tympanum directly above, sits the Virgin,

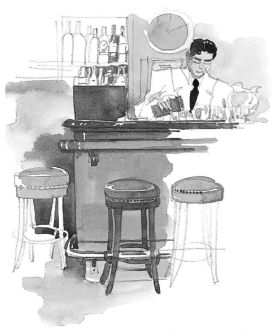

The barmen of Harry's Bar jealously guard their customer's secrets... as well as the recipe for Bellinis, the best in the world!

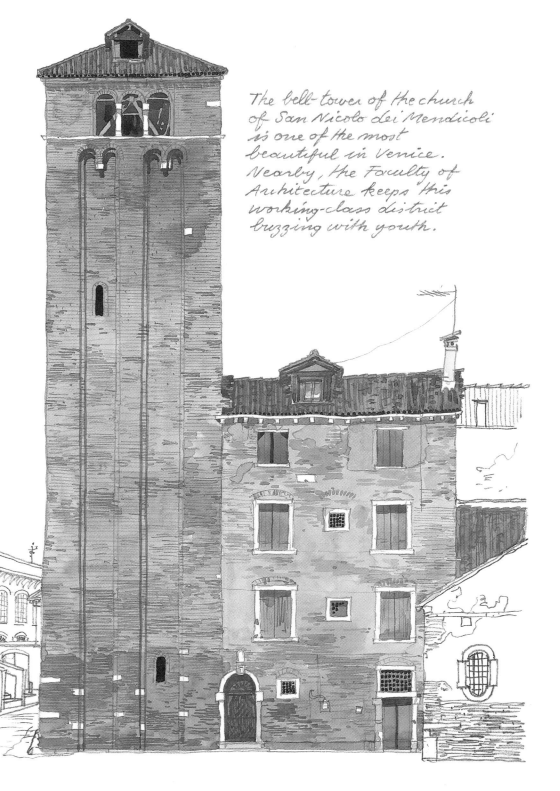

The bell-tower of the church of San Nicolo dei Mendicoli is one of the most beautiful in Venice. Nearby, the Faculty of Architecture keeps this working-class district buzzing with youth.

one of many statues which enliven the façades. Sixteen gigantic scrolls counterbalance the buttresses that support the dome. Inside, a walkway delineates the octagonal central section. Two semi-circular apses flank the high altar, towards which all eyes should converge. The polychrome marble paving, flooded with light, reflects the structure of the building and radiates out from the inscription in the middle to the six side chapels.

Palazzo Dario
Palazzo Dario was built at the end of the 15th century for Giovanni Dario, Secretary of the Senate of the Republic at the Sultan's court in Constantinople. Given the quality of the polychrome marble facing, the building is generally attributed to Pietro Lombardo and his workshop. The façade overlooking the garden, however, is Gothic.

Campo Santa Margherita
This is one of the largest and most popular squares in Venice. Its great size is due to the fact that the surrounding canals were covered over in the middle of the 19th century. The truncated bell-tower of the former church of the same name is now inhabited.

Ponte dei Pugni
The Bridge of Fists, formerly without parapets, was the scene of many confrontations between two rival factions: the Nicolotti from Dorsoduro, with their berets and black scarves, and the Arsenalotti from Castello, also with berets but with red scarves. However, in 1705, these 'games' were prohibited, said to be too dangerous. The bridge still bears the footprints of the protagonists.

San Pantalon
This church was rebuilt by Francesco Comino in the second half of the 17th century on top of the foundations of a much smaller church dating from the 13th century. Its façade was never completed. The enormous vault (900 m²) is literally coated with canvases (sixty in all) by Gian Antonio Fumiani, painted between 1680 and 1704, illustrating the life of St Pantalon, a doctor martyred by the Emperor Diocletian for having converted to Catholicism.

San Barnaba
The Church of San Barnaba, built by Lorenzo Boschetti in 1749, has a Neo-classical façade. Abandoned for a long while, the church now houses an exhibition of sacred objects.

San Trovaso boatyard
This is the oldest surviving boatyard in Venice, unique in its architecture, typical of the wooden chalets in Cadore, from whence came not only the craftsmen who made the boats here, but also the wood to make them with. A century ago, there were still plenty of *squeri* (boatyards) – the word derives from *squadra* (set-square), an indispensable tool for ship-building. In 1610, the artisans formed a congregation, with their altar in the nearby Church of San Trovaso (an abbreviation of Gervasio and Protasio). Rebuilt in 1589 and heavily influenced by the work of Palladio, San Trovaso is the only church in Venice with two identical façades.

Palazzo Venier dei Leoni
Begun in 1749 by Lorenzo Boschetti, this building was designed to be every bit as monumental and grand as its contemporary, Palazzo Grassi. The imposing wooden model housed in the Correr Museum gives an idea of the intended size of the palazzo which, due to pressure from the powerful Correr family on the opposite side of the Grand Canal, never rose higher than the ground floor. After the Second World War, Peggy Guggenheim moved into this ashlar-facaded, white Istrian stone building which today houses her contemporary art collection.

Emporio del Sale
These were warehouses for storing salt, once one of the Serenissima's most lucrative industries. They were rebuilt by Giovanni Alvise Pigazzi in 1830. Today they are the headquarters of the association Canottieri Bucintoro.

Rio Terrà dei Catecumeni
Covered over in the middle of the 19th century, this canal took its name from the neighbouring hospice built in 1571 to house the slaves and prisoners who wished to become Christians. Rebuilt by Giorgio Massari in 1727, it is now a convent for Salesian nuns who provide lodging for female students.

San Nicolo dei Mendicoli

Legend has it that the Church of San Nicolo dei Mendicoli was built on the ruins of a Roman temple dedicated to Venus, as shown in the paintings on the ceiling. The groundplan with its central nave is left over from the original 7th-century construction. Altered and added to on numerous occasions between the 12th and 14th centuries, the church is built of brick and has conserved its 15th-century porch on the main façade, a typical feature of Venetian architecture of the period. The church's name, St Nicholas of the Beggars, derives from the fact that this district used to be one of the poorest in Venice.

Il Redentore

The Church of the Redentore, built between 1577 and 1592, was designed by Andrea Palladio and completed after his death by his disciple, Vincenzo Scamozzi. This imposing sanctuary was intended to exorcise the devastating plague of 1575. Inside, the curvilinear forms accentuate and link the different parts of the building: the central nave, the side chapels, the presbytery with its cupola, the choir. Light streams into the church, reflecting off the paving. The central nave is all reds and whites, while the presbytery, with its semi-circular apses reserved for officiating clergy and notables, is lavishly adorned with grey, black, white and pink marble. The Redentore is one of the few projects by Palladio to have survived unaltered. Following the austere rules of the Capucin order, the Senate forbade, amongst other things, the addition of any funerary monuments, thus preserving the architectural purity of the edifice.

The Church of the Zitelle

Designed by Andrea Palladio, the Church of the Zitelle and the convent which surrounds it on three sides, were built by Jacopo Bozzetto between 1582 and 1586. Originally called Santa Maria della Presentazione, the church has a square floorplan, almost entirely covered by a dome. The façade is made up of two bell-towers flanking a semi-circular bay topped by a tympanum.

Mulino Stucky

Commissioned by the Swiss entrepreneur Giovanni Stucky, and constructed by the German architect Ernest Wullekopf in 1896, the massive Neo-Gothic brick silhouette of the Mulino Stucky dominates the Giudecca canal. Until 1954, it was a flourmill and pasta factory; it then fell into disuse for a long while, and is only now being restored by the architect Francesco Amendolaggine.

Corte dei Cordami, Giudecca

In this picturesque district of the Giudecca, the gaily painted houses are built around a courtyard perpendicular to the canal, where once there were gardens. Formerly used to make rope for shipping, the houses had large chimneys constructed on the outside to reduce the risk of fire.

San Giorgio Maggiore

The Benedictine monastery founded on this island in 982 has since become a place of great spirituality. Kitchen gardens, vineyards and other buildings gradually grew up around it. One of the two cloisters and the dormitory, 128 m in length and known as Manica Lunga, were built by Giovanni Buora and his son Andrea in the 15th century. Palladio worked here from 1566 until his death in 1580, giving it its present look. He designed the refectory, where Veronese painted *The Wedding at Cana* (today in the Louvre Museum in Paris), the second cloister and the church, all completed by Simone Sorella in 1612. Longhena was responsible for the library between 1641 and 1653. In spite of its unusual length, the church appears to be centrered around the intersection of the nave and the transepts, above which towers the dome. Dominating the entire lagoon, the façade is punctuated by four columns and a triangular pediment. There is the most magnificent view from the top of the bell-tower, built in 1726 by Scalfarotto: the whole of Venice and its surroundings as far as the eye can see.

San Michele

Since the Napoleonic decree of 1807, the island of San Michele has been the public cemetery of Venice. Covering almost the entire island, it was constructed between 1872 and 1881 by Annibale Forcellini. Numerous famous artists lie at rest in the shade of its cypress trees: Diaghilev, Stravinsky, Ezra Pound, Luigi Nono...

Murano

Santi Maria e Donato is part of one of the lagoon's large religious settlements, founded in the 7th century, remodelled after the year AD 1000 along the lines of a basilica. The apse is a masterpiece of late 12th-century Veneto-Byzantine art, with its double row of small arcades resting on twin columns, its splayed niches and balustrades. Inside, fantastic creatures, eagles and fish from the mid-12th century intertwine on the mosaic floor. The architect and author Camillo Boito, brother of Arrigo, Verdi's librettist, contributed to the restoration of the church from 1859 to 1873. Overlooking the canal lies Palazzo Trevisan, a masterpiece of the Renaissance, decorated with Veronese frescoes. On the other side of the canal, in the 17th-century Palazzo Giustinian, is the glass museum.

Burano

The 16th-century Church of San Martino overlooks the main square, its bell-tower leaning perilously, next to the Gothic Palazzo Podestà, which now houses the Museo del Merletto (lace museum). Burano has been known for its lacemaking throughout the world since the 17th century. The square and the main street are named after the musician Baldassare Galuppi (1706-1785), native of Burano and nicknamed 'Il Buranello'.

Torcello

Until the 10th century, this peaceful island was a burgeoning city. Basilica Santa Maria Assunta, founded in the 7th century, was altered during the 9th and 11th centuries. The typical triple-nave basilical plan, punctuated by marble columns, shows the influence of the late Roman period, while the mosaics inside, from the Veneto-Byzantine school, are quite exceptional. Nearby, lies the 11th-century Church of Santa Fosca, the lagoon's sole example of Byzantine architecture. It is an octagonal-shaped church built on a plan in the shape of a Greek cross, surrounded on five sides by an arcade with finely sculpted capitals. It originally served as a martyrium (housing a saint's tomb) for the Basilica and is linked to it via this arcade.

San Francesco del Deserto

This church was built in 1228 by Jacopo Michiel, in memory of St Francis of Assisi, who stopped here on his return from the Holy Land in 1220. It was subsequently donated to the Franciscans who added a monastery with a beautiful cloister. Abandoned in the 15th century because of an outbreak of malaria,

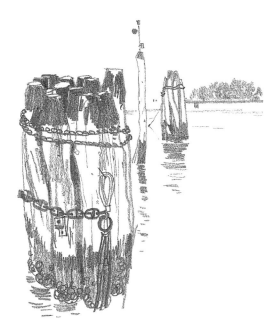

the island was once again settled by monks in the 19th century. A few years ago, it became a place for spiritual retreats.

The Lido

12 km long, the island of Lido is a well-known seaside resort. All that remains of the original 10th-century Church San Nicolo del Lido are two capitals and a few fragments of paving. The church was rebuilt in 1662, but its façade was never completed. The elegant Renaissance cloister dates from 1530.

Pellestrina

The *murazzi*, the vast Istrian stone dykes, 4 km long and 14 m wide, were built by the mathematician Bernardino Zendrini, based on a plan by Father Vincenzo Coronelli. The construction began in 1744 and lasted 34 years. Today, it is these same *murazzi* which protect the long strip of land that separates the lagoon from the Adriatic Sea, part of which forms the island of Pellestrina. At its centre, the polygonal Church of Santa Maria di San Vito rises up, built in 1716 by Andrea Tirali in honour of the Virgin to thank her for saving the island from Turkish invasion.

Chioggia

To the extreme south of the lagoon lies Chioggia, a former Roman port, and the European salt capital during the Middle Ages. Its cathedral, founded in the 11th century in honour of Our Lady of the Assumption, was destroyed by fire in 1623 and rebuilt by Baldassare Longhena in 1633.

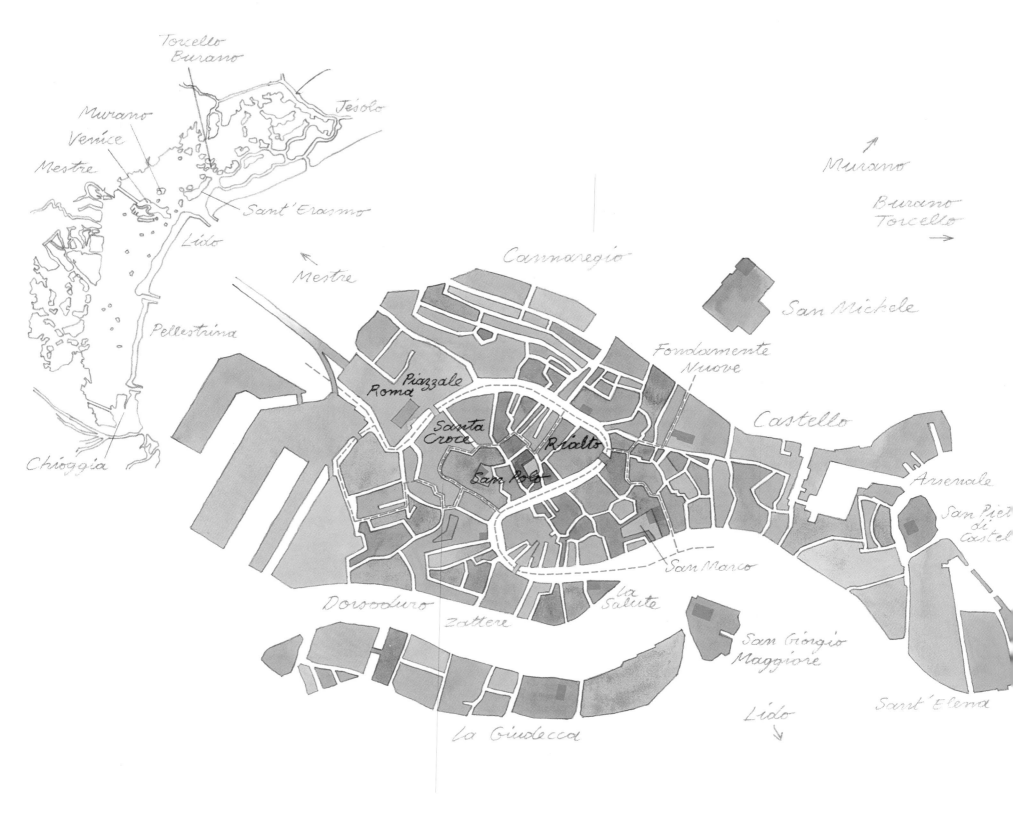

Torcello
Burano

Murano
Venice

Mestre

Jesolo

Sant'Erasmo

Lido

Pellestrina

Chioggia

Murano

Burano
Torcello

Cannaregio

San Michele

Mestre

Fondamente
Nuove

Castello

Piazzale
Roma

Santa
Croce

Rialto

San Polo

San Marco

Arsenale

San Pietro
di
Castello

Dorsoduro

Zattere

la
Salute

San Giorgio
Maggiore

Sant'Elena

La Giudecca

Lido